Donald Davie was born in Barnsley, England, in 1922. "My formal education, interrupted by war service," he writes, "was at Cambridge. In a deeper sense, nothing was more educational than eighteen months in Arctic Russia, 1942–43, and seven years, 1950–57, in the city of Dublin." He has taught at the University of Dublin, at Cambridge, at the University of Southern California, and elsewhere, and is currently in the English Department at Stanford University. Books by him include his *Collected Poems, 1950–1970*, *Thomas Hardy and British Poetry*, and *Ezra Pound: Poet as Sculptor*.

Frank Kermode, King Edward VII Professor of English Literature at Cambridge, is the author of *The Classic; D. H. Lawrence; Shakespeare, Spenser, Donne;* and other widely acclaimed critical studies.

MODERN MASTERS

ALBERT CAMUS / Conor Cruise O'Brien
FRANTZ FANON / David Caute
HERBERT MARCUSE / Alasdair MacIntyre
CHE GUEVARA / Andrew Sinclair
LUDWIG WITTGENSTEIN / David Pears
GEORGE LUKÁCS / George Lichtheim
NOAM CHOMSKY / John Lyons
JAMES JOYCE / John Gross
MARSHALL MCLUHAN / Jonathan Miller
GEORGE ORWELL / Raymond Williams
SIGMUND FREUD / Richard Wollheim
WILLIAM BUTLER YEATS / Denis Donoghue
WILHELM REICH / Charles Rycroft
MOHANDAS GANDHI / George Woodcock
BERTRAND RUSSELL / A. J. Ayer
NORMAN MAILER / Richard Poirier
V. I. LENIN / Robert Conquest
EINSTEIN / Jeremy Bernstein

ALREADY PUBLISHED

C. G. JUNG / Anthony Storr
D. H. LAWRENCE / Frank Kermode
KARL POPPER / Bryan Magee
SAMUEL BECKETT / A. Alvarez
R. D. LAING / Edgar Z. Friedenberg
MAX WEBER / Donald G. MacRae
MARCEL PROUST / Roger Shattuck
LE CORBUSIER / Stephen Gardiner
CLAUDE LEVI-STRAUSS (*Rev. Ed.*) / Edmund Leach
ARNOLD SCHOENBERG / Charles Rosen
FRANZ KAFKA / Erich Heller
KARL MARX / David McLellan
JEAN-PAUL SARTRE / Arthur C. Danto
T. S. ELIOT / Stephen Spender
EZRA POUND / Donald Davie
JOHN MAYNARD KEYNES / D. E. Moggridge
FERDINAND DE SAUSSURE / Jonathan Culler

PENGUIN
MODERN MASTERS

EDITED BY frank kermode

By Modern Masters we mean the men who
have changed and are changing the life and
thought of our age. The authors of these volumes are themselves masters, and they have
written their books in the belief that general
discussion of their subjects will henceforth be
more informed and more exciting than ever
before.   —F.K.

ezra
pound

donald davie

PENGUIN BOOKS

Penguin Books Ltd, Harmondsworth, Middlesex, England
Penguin Books, 625 Madison Avenue, New York, New York 10022, U.S.A.
Penguin Books Australia Ltd, Ringwood, Victoria, Australia
Penguin Books Canada Ltd, 41 Steelcase Road West, Markham, Ontario, Canada
Penguin Books (N.Z.) Ltd, 182–190 Wairau Road, Auckland 10, New Zealand

First published in Great Britain by Fontana 1975
Published in the United States of America by The Viking Press 1976
Published in Penguin Books 1976

LIBRARY OF CONGRESS CATALOGING IN PUBLICATION DATA
Davie, Donald.
Ezra Pound.
(Penguin modern masters)
British ed. published in 1975 under title: Pound.
Bibliography: p.
Includes index.
1. Pound, Ezra Loomis, 1885–1972—Criticism and interpretation.
[PS3531.082Z582   1976b]   811'.5'2   76-27980
ISBN 0 14 00.4318 7 (pbk.)

Printed in the United States of America by
Offset Paperback Mfrs., Inc., Dallas, Pennsylvania
Set in Linotype Primer

Acknowledgment is made to the following for permission to use material:
Macmillan Publishing Co., Inc.: "The Voice" from *Collected Poems* of Thomas
Hardy. Copyright 1925 by Macmillan Publishing Co., Inc.
New Directions Publishing Corp.: *A Lume Spento*, Copyright © 1965 by Ezra
Pound. All rights reserved. *Personae*, Copyright 1926 by Ezra Pound. *The
Cantos*, Copyright 1937, 1948, © 1956, 1959, 1962, 1966, 1970 by Ezra Pound,
Literary Essays, Copyright 1918, 1920, 1935 by Ezra Pound. *Guide to Kul-
chur*, Copyright © 1970 by Ezra Pound. All Rights Reserved. *The Spirit of
Romance*, Copyright © 1968 by Ezra Pound. All Rights Reserved. *Confucius to
Cummings*, Copyright © 1964 by New Directions Publishing Corporation.
Selected Prose, Copyright © 1960, 1962 by Ezra Pound. Copyright © 1973 by
The Estate of Ezra Pound. *Patria Mia*, Copyright © 1950 by Ralph Fletcher
Seymour. "Three Letters to Thomas Hardy," Copyright © 1968 by the Trustees
for the Ezra Pound Literary Property Trust. Reprinted by permission of New
Directions Publishing Corporation.

CONTENTS

		Biographical Note	viii
		Introduction	1
i	/	Romance Languages	11
ii	/	A Programmatic Decade	27
iii	/	*Hugh Selwyn Mauberley* and *Homage to Sextus Propertius*	43
iv	/	Ideas in *The Cantos*	62
v	/	Rhythms in *The Cantos*	77
vi	/	Toward a Conclusion	99
		Conclusion	118
		Short Bibliography	121
		Index	127

BIOGRAPHICAL NOTE

1885   Ezra Loomis Pound born October 10 in Hailey, Idaho. But Pound grew up in a suburb of Philadelphia.

1898   First visit to Europe (Venice), accompanying his great-aunt.

1901–05   Studies at the University of Pennsylvania under Hugo Rennert, and at Hamilton College under William Pierce Shepherd.

1906   M.A., University of Pennsylvnia. Awarded a Harrison fellowship, and revisits Europe, working on Lope de Vega.

1907   Instructor in French and Spanish at Wabash College, Crawfordsville, Indiana.

1908   Travels to Italy, where *A Lume Spento* is published in Venice, and then to London, where he makes his home and meets W. B. Yeats, Ford Madox Ford, and others.

1914   Marries Dorothy Shakespear, meets T. S. Eliot, and contributes to Wyndham Lewis's *Blast*.

1920   Moves to Paris and lives there until 1924, asso-
            ciating with Brancusi, Joyce, Hemingway, Coc-
            teau, and others.

1926   Pound's opera, *The Testament of François Villon*,
            performed in Paris.

1928   Settles in Rapallo, Italy.

1935   Publishes *Social Credit: An Impact*, and other
            pamphlets on international politics and finance.

1939   Visits the United States (for the first time since
            1910); receives an honorary degree from Hamil-
            ton College.

1940   Begins to broadcast from Rome.

1941   The United States declares war on the Axis pow-
            ers. Pound discontinues his broadcasts, but then
            resumes them.

1942   Attempts without success to join Americans be-
            ing evacuated from Italy.

1943   Indicted for treason *in absentia*, in Washington.

1945   Handed over by Italian partisans to the U.S.
            Army, and confined in the U.S. Army Discipli-
            nary Training Centre near Pisa. In November, is
            sent by air to Washington, D.C., for treason trial.

1946   Found medically unfit to stand trial, is committed
            to St. Elizabeths Hospital for the Criminally In-
            sane, Washington, D.C.

1948   Dorothy Pound permitted to come to Washington
            to be her husband's companion.

1949   Pound awarded Bollingen Award for Poetry, for *The
            Pisan Cantos*; the award provokes bitter controversy.

1958   The indictment for treason dismissed, is released
            from St. Elizabeths, and returns to Italy to di-
            vide his time between Rapallo, Venice, and his
            daughter's home near Merano.

1965   Visits London for the funeral of T. S. Eliot, and
            Dublin to call on the widow of W. B. Yeats.

1969   Briefly revisits the United States.

1972   Dies November 1 in Venice.

IN MEMORIAM E.L.P.

A midland
        peninsular light
"Mediterranean"
          hugs the white stucco

        and heat
rises, rearing up from cool dawn and earth
into its midday passion
         for precise description;

leaves mesh like knives
or woven wire,
narrow black shadows lie scattered in a prison
of limbs and leaves

and recall other places,
recall the effect of other places

on the traveller, striding through Spain
and southern France, whose works

lie on the shelf
like a basket of lemons and stones.

—Reginald Gibbons
CALIFORNIA, 1973

INTRODUCTION

Ezra Loomis Pound, for some years before he died in Venice in 1972, had figured, for those few who took note of such careers as his, in the appealing role of "the lone survivor." He had outlived everyone of those with whom he had been associated in the international avant-garde of the twentieth century. Henri Gaudier-Brzeska and Jacob Epstein and Constantin Brancusi; Percy Wyndham Lewis and George Antheil and T. E. Hulme; William Butler Yeats and James Joyce; Jean Cocteau and Francis Picabia; T. S. Eliot and William Carlos Williams and Ernest Hemingway—each of those names (and the list could be extended almost infinitely) had achieved fame or had attracted notoriety. Pound, who knew them all, survived them all. And his strategy for handling the condition of survivor which chance or fate had wished upon him was striking: it was silence. Quite literally, silence. He rose, properly and indeed nobly, to obituary occasions, as in a tribute to his longtime friend, rival, and at times almost-enemy T. S. Eliot. But, for the most part, as we know from numerous accounts of visitors to his last home in Venice, his response to interrogations, or even to increasingly random and distraught conversational gambits, was silence. He had nothing to say; or else, whatever was worth saying he had said already; or else again—and this came nearer to the painful truth—he no longer trusted himself to say anything, because too much of what he had said seemed to him now to be dangerously false.

For the last sustained statement that Pound made about his own life and work, before he took what looks like a vow of silence, was an interview which he gave in 1963 to Grazia Levi, representing the Italian journal *Epoca*, where the interview subsequently appeared. It includes this exchange:

POUND: . . . For myself, I know that I do not know anything. . . .

LEVI: But when you were writing *A Lume Spento* and *Lustra*, or when you were studying Confucius, or when you labored over the tremendous scope of *The Cantos*, you had a feeling of certainty?

POUND: Oh, yes indeed I had it! In fact, I repeat: I have come too late to the consciousness of doubt.

LEVI: But if this great doubt had come to you earlier, how would it have directed your life, your work?

POUND: I would have avoided so many errors! My aims were good, but I blundered in the method of attaining them. I have been stupid like a telescope seen through the wrong end. Too late came the understanding. . . . Too late came the uncertainty of knowing nothing. . . .

LEVI: What is it, now, that holds you to life, from the time that you have acquired a total certainty of uncertainty?

POUND: Nothing holds me any longer to life. . . .[1]

This pleased nobody. On the one hand, no one of the many who had maintained over the years that Pound was a self-deluded ignoramus applauded this costly confession by the poet that that was indeed in part how he saw himself; and, on the other hand, the many poets and critics of poetry who by 1963 had invested heavily in the essential rightness of Pound's poetic theory and practice could not afford to believe the poet when he told them the stock they had invested in was unsound. Thus Louis Dudek, whose translation from the Italian I have been quoting, had to remind his Canadian readers that "Pound is now seventy-eight years old. He has suffered from several paralytic strokes, and has recently recovered somewhat from a very serious illness."

But it will not do thus to hint that Pound at seventy-eight was too weak and bewildered for his pronouncements to carry weight. Not only did he deliver himself in a similar strain to other interrogators[2] but it was thus that he expressed himself in his last published poems:

Tho' my errors and wrecks lie about me.
And I am not a demigod,
I cannot make it cohere. . . .

---

[1] *Delta* (Canada) Vol. 22 (October, 1963), 3–4.
[2] See Daniel Cory, "Ezra Pound. A Memoir," *Encounter*, Vol. 30, no. 5 (1968).

Also:

> *Many errors,*
> *a little rightness . . .*

And:

> *To confess wrong without losing rightness:*
> *Charity I have had sometimes,*
> *I cannot make it flow thru. . . .*

These passages from Canto 116 (first published between hard covers in 1967) show clearly that Louis Dudek was right to protest when a Reuter's dispatch glossed the interview in *Epoca* as: "He said he regretted everything he had written." But in Pound at the end of his life we certainly have a modern master who accuses himself bitterly and in all seriousness of having, through ignorance and impetuosity, botched too much of what he set out to do. As it happens, I agree with Dudek that Pound in these dispirited comments was being much too hard on himself; but there certainly *were* botches, and it is only right that the reader be told to look out for them.

Pound's admirers have gone to great pains to brush these late self-accusations under the carpet, or to explain them away. Yet for Pound thus to accuse himself is surely admirable. He had been accused repeatedly; for him to admit the justice of at least some of the accusations seems greatly to his credit. To take only the most blatant and damaging of the charges, concerning his anti-Semitism, should we not respect him for admitting, however belatedly, "the worst mistake I made was that stupid, suburban prejudice of anti-Semitism?"[3] It appears not. On the contrary, one gets the clear impres-

[3] Michael Reck, "A Conversation between Ezra Pound and Allen Ginsberg," *Evergreen Review*, 57 (June, 1968).

sion that for Pound to confess his faults is almost worse than having committed them. The lines of battle are drawn: one is in favor of modernism or else against it; and for Pound, marshaled in the front rank of modernism, to waver in his place even for a moment is profoundly demoralizing for ally and adversary alike.

This may suggest that "the modern" is by no means such a single and simple phenomenon as we like to suppose; that on the contrary an accredited champion of the modern like Pound turns out, when one looks, to be in all sorts of ways strikingly old-fashioned; and equally that the self-appointed spokesmen of "the traditional" may turn out to have less rights in that "tradition" than a figure like Pound has.

Ezra Pound—or, as we are learning to say almost without embarrassment, Pound Studies—is a major industry, internationally. If the Eliot industry and the Joyce industry got off the ground earlier than the Pound enterprise, the last, it now seems certain, will outstrip its forerunners in the sheer quantity of printed words it will provoke. For Pound, unlike Joyce and Eliot, was a spendthrift—of time, of energy, of feeling, of opinion; and so the researchers will be kept busy through scores of years, not pointlessly busy either, since the material that has to be unearthed, scrutinized, and classified is vast and various. This throws a queer light on those Poundians—Marshall McLuhan for one, Max Nänny for another—who have argued that Pound's significance lies in his having anticipated the end of "the Gutenberg era," the age of print.[4] The plain fact is that Pound's life

[4] Max Nänny, *Ezra Pound: Poetics for an Electric Age* (Bern, 1973).

and writings have stimulated print, acres of it, and will certainly stimulate much more! Shall we be told that this is a transitional phenomenon, the Gutenberg era exerting itself with unprecedented vigor precisely so as to encompass a phenomenon which in fact transcends it, and so signals its end? That may be the case. The short-term effects are nonetheless sourly comical—the man who deplored the industrialization of scholarship, himself furnishes the raw material for scholarly industry on a grand scale; the man who distrusted the proliferation of printed pages is himself the pretext for many more such pages; the man who delivered his sense of things characteristically in terse apothegm and racy aphorism is himself treated of in deliberate treatises at pedestrian length.

Rather few of these pages have concerned themselves with the humble but necessary and honorable task of establishing the facts of who Pound was, where he was (and with whom) on such and such a day in such and such a year, how he behaved on occasions when we know he was present. Two books,[5] and a few sparse and scattered essays, concern themselves with information of this kind. Most of the operatives in the Pound factory have unfortunately more grandiose objectives; and so nothing like a definitive biography can be expected for

[5] Charles Norman's *Ezra Pound: A Biography* has been superseded by Noel Stock, *The Life of Ezra Pound*, which is however far from definitive. Among studies of limited periods of Pound's life, of which one must hope for many more, are Patricia Hutchins, *Ezra Pound's Kensington* (London, 1965) and Harry M. Meacham, *The Caged Panther: Ezra Pound at St. Elizabeths* (New York, 1967). Since 1972, the journal *Paideuma*, published from the University of Maine at Orono, has been exclusively concerned with collecting information about Pound, some of it biographical.

many years. By the same token, many of Pound's most challenging comments on modern civilization lie buried in the files of defunct magazines, from which no one seems eager to rescue them. It is even true that "the state of the text of Pound's work, both poetry and prose, is a disgrace." In the years since 1967, when Eric Homberger pointed this out,[6] no start has been made on putting it right.

Because of this cavalier disregard of ascertainable facts and documents we can be offered, as a portrait of the youthful Pound, a figure who "was seeking a radical redefinition of poetic possibilities and returning to the roots of civilization in order to show how much had been lost in the watery conventions handed over to us by the nineteenth century."[7] The ascertainable records present us on the contrary with a man who admired Swinburne and Thomas Hardy and D. G. Rossetti, Beddoes and Landor and Browning, Gautier and Heine and Leopardi, Stendhal and Remy de Gourmont and Flaubert; a man who had virtually no views of American nineteenth-century literature, since he appears not to have read attentively (nor was he to read) Emily Dickinson or Melville or Hawthorne, Fenimore Cooper or Thoreau; who thought on the other hand that "there is more wisdom, perhaps more 'revolution' in Whistler's portrait of young Miss Alexander than in all the Judaic drawings of the 'prophetic' Blake";[8] in short, a man who

---

[6] Eric Homberger, "Ezra Pound and the Ostriches," *Cambridge Review*, Vol. 89, no. 2156 (November 1967).

[7] George Quasha, *Open Poetry. Four Anthologies of Expanded Poems . . .* (New York, 1972), Introduction.

[8] *Ezra Pound: Selected Prose 1909–1965*, William Cookson, ed., p. 418; reprinted from "Remy de Gourmont," *Fortnightly Review*, xcviii (n.s.), 1915.

carried more nineteenth-century baggage than any comparably gifted contemporary among writers in English. If Pound is a master and founding father of twentieth-century modernism in the arts, it is certainly not by virtue of having exploded, and persuaded us to reject, nineteenth-century pretensions.

We may reach back further, and consider not the nineteenth century but the eighteenth, as it comes to a close for English-speakers in the figure of William Blake, that English engraver and visionary poet whom Pound once thought so manifestly inferior to James McNeill Whistler. Yet there are those who would make Pound and Blake two of a kind. One of them says of Blake: "He sought a level of transformation that would feed back into life, partly by exposing the ways that art and culture generally played into the hands of a diseased civilization, and partly by offering actual models of spiritual expansion."[9] But the eighteenth-century civilization which Blake's poems allegedly expose as "diseased" had nourished Henry Fielding and George Crabbe, Voltaire and Fontenelle and Metastasio, John Adams and Thomas Jefferson, all of them men whom Pound approved or applauded. As with nineteenth-century "romantic" culture, so with eighteenth-century "Enlightenment" culture, we find Pound cast in a role of iconoclast which an unprejudiced scrutiny of his recorded opinions simply will not support.

Accordingly, when we hear it happily declared of the United States in the 1970s, "Our scene is very different from the cultural vacuum at the turn of the century which drove Ezra Pound heroically to seek to 'resusci-

[9] Quasha, *loc. cit.*

tate the dead art of poetry,'" we ought to be on our guard. And sure enough the documents make it clear that, for the young Ezra Pound, London between 1908 and 1912 was anything but a "cultural vacuum," if only because it contained the author of *The Wind among the Reeds*, and the author of *The Ambassadors*, and the author of *Under the Greenwood Tree*,[10] and Ford Madox Ford and T. E. Hulme, not to mention others whom Pound admired, like Frederic Manning and G. R. S. Mead and Allen Upward. Moreover, many readers of Pound's *Hugh Selwyn Mauberley* take the line, "resuscitate the dead art of poetry," ironically, as a gibe at anyone who is damfool enough to think that the art of poetry is, or could be, "dead." In short, everywhere we turn, so long as we have some scruples about evidence, we encounter in the young Pound not a revolutionary or iconoclast but a sometimes militant conservative.

Indeed, it is possible to argue that Pound was at bottom an Edwardian man of letters like Edmund Gosse or George Saintsbury, and that the provocative oddities of his later poetry and his later opinions reflect merely the increasingly desperate straits to which a man formed in that milieu was compelled, as political and social developments destroyed any possibility of that kind of milieu being reconstituted. Certainly Pound's Edwardianism, if we may call it that, was something that he never wholly outgrew. And so when he died, there disappeared not only the last surviving specimen of one sort of twentieth-century modernist but also, odd as it must seem, the last survivor of a still older breed, formed by the century before.

[10] Respectively, W. B. Yeats, Henry James, and Thomas Hardy.

Romance Languages

i

Nothing could be more genteel, or less iconoclastic in its tone and implications, than Pound's subtitle to his first prose book, *The Spirit of Romance* (1910): *An Attempt to Define Somewhat the Charm of the Pre-Renaissance Literature of Latin Europe* ("by Ezra Pound, M.A., Author of *Personae* and *Exultations*"). "Somewhat" and "charm" are such worlds away from the brutally emphatic language of Pound's later prose that we are tempted to think this title page was composed tongue-in-cheek. But there is no evidence of that. On the contrary, if we're to pick up Pound at the start of his career we have to transport ourselves into a climate where "somewhat" and "charm" and indeed "romance" are part of the vocabulary with which serious

and accomplished people address themselves to serious
questions about culture.

Moreover, the ground that Pound covers in this book,
as he had in public lectures in London in 1908–09 and
again in 1909–10—Bion and Moschus from ancient
Sicily, the Provençal troubadours, *The Song of Roland*
and *Poema del Cid*, the *dolce stil nuovo* and Dante,
Villon, Lope de Vega, Camoëns, Latin poets of the
Renaissance—is thoroughly in line with such a monu-
ment of Edwardian literary culture as George Saintsbury's *Periods of European Literature*. As epigraph to the
twelve volumes of this encyclopedic work stands a
quotation from Matthew Arnold:

> The criticism which alone can help us for the future
> is a criticism which regards Europe as being, for
> intellectual and spiritual purposes, one great con-
> federation, bound to a joint action and working to a
> common result.

But when Saintsbury in 1907 gets to his twelfth volume,
and is compelled to notice some Russian and Polish and
Scandinavian authors, he does so with marked impa-
tience and distaste, and we see that "Europe," as conceived by Saintsbury following Arnold's directive, is not
the same as the geographical entity thus named, but
something much smaller, centered on the Mediterranean and in effect comprising only the area of the
Romance languages, though English and German are
allowed in as special cases. And this seems to be true
also of Pound—not only of the young scholar who published *The Spirit of Romance*, and in 1906 had been a
graduate fellow of the University of Pennsylvania, his
field the Romance languages; but also of the Pound who

in the 1920s confessed to Ernest Hemingway, "To tell the truth, Hem, I've never read the Rooshians"; and even of the Pound who, after two world wars had broken over Europe, was to write from a prison camp (Canto 76):

> *As a lone ant from a broken ant-hill*
> *from the wreckage of Europe, ego scriptor.*

The European "confederation" that Pound thought he spoke for throughout his life was effectively a Europe that spoke Latin and its Romance derivatives, including English as the most remote and partial of those derivatives, and making special provision for classical Greek as in important ways the original source of them all, even of Latin. And the sanities and wisdoms that Pound conceived of himself as promoting against the ever-more impudent barbarians were carried—so he thought, and was to think—pre-eminently in Latin and the Romance languages: Italian, Spanish, French (and, when he remembered, Portuguese). What looks like a glaring exception to this rule—Pound's enthusiasm for Chinese language and culture—is far more apparent than real, as we shall see. Such a prejudice or predisposition was more common in Saintsbury's generation than it has been since, when Dostoevski and Nietzsche, Freud and Ibsen and Frantz Fanon have increasingly jostled Arnaud Daniel and François Villon for the attention of people who aspire to be well-read. And coming at it from this point of view, we see it was no accident that when the time came for Pound like most of his contemporaries to swerve into political aberrations, it should have been Italian fascism that trapped him, not German National Socialism or Russian communism.

But if the language trusted by the young Pound is
Romance language in this respectable, technical, and
well-defined sense, what's to be said of language like
this?

> *Aye, I am wistful for my kin of the spirit*
> *And have none about me save in the shadows*
> *When come they, surging of power, 'DAEMON'*
> *'Quasi KALOUN'. S.T. says Beauty is most that, a*
> *   'calling to the soul.'*
> *Well then, so call they, the swirlers out of the mist of*
> *   my soul,*
> *They that come mewards, bearing old magic.*

Here we have "Romance language" in an altogether less
reputable sense, which has more to do with romanticism
(and with Victorian late-romanticism) than with the
harshly direct language of a genuine "Romance" poet
like Villon. The lines above are from "In Durance"
(1907), which appeared in Pound's third collection,
Personae (London 1909); and what they are struggling
to say is after a fashion in keeping with the language
that Pound tries to say it in. "S.T." is Coleridge, and the
Coleridge text appealed to is the essay "On the Principles of Genial Criticism," which advances a Platonic or
neo-Platonic idea of the nature and function of poetry,
as Pound's poem does also. Moreover, the neo-Platonic
matter of these lines is something that persisted in
Pound's thought. And if, as historians of ideas, we were
to concentrate on the paraphrasable content of Pound's
poetry, we could see such an early poem as saying
things which he will still be saying at the end of his life.
But it is precisely the radical difference in the manner
of saying, early and late, which is crucial. For the experience of reading Pound's *Cantos* isn't remotely like

the experience of reading neo-Platonic romantic poets like Shelley or D. G. Rossetti. So what is the point of establishing that if Pound had written differently he might have sounded like the Shelley who wrote *Epipsychidion*? The historian of ideas may be interested but the reader of poetry is not, nor should he be. What he needs to attend to is the Foreword that Pound supplied in 1964 when he allowed his very first collection, *A Lume Spento* (originally Venice, 1908), to be reprinted:

> As to why a reprint? No lessons to be learned save the depth of ignorance, or rather the superficiality of non-perception—neither eye nor ear. Ignorance that didn't know the meaning of "Wardour Street."

Who knows that meaning now? The expression was more current in 1908 than in 1964. In 1976 we need a dictionary:

> The name of a street in London, mainly occupied by dealers in antique and imitation-antique furniture . . . applied to the pseudo-archaic diction affected by some writers, esp. of historical novels, 1888.

"Pseudo-archaic" is exact for "Aye, I am wistful," and "They that come mewards." Whole books were written in this excruciating idiom, notably by Pound's English friend Maurice Hewlett, who shared his enthusiasm for medieval Aquitaine of the troubadours. This is romance language in the sense that it is the language of historical romances written in late-Victorian and Edwardian England; it is not a medium in which anything can be communicated forcefully or crisply.

This is, however, only one component in the language

of these lines. "Surging of power" belongs in some different idiom altogether, which is impossible to name;
the notetaker's telegraphese of "S.T." belongs in another
idiom again; and the Greek expressions, "DAEMON"
and "Quasi KALOUN," belong in yet another. These last
are syntactically quite without anchorage in what offers
itself as a normal English sentence. And this abandon-
ment of grammar mirrors accurately the desperation of
the poet, who can manage no more than to have these
disparate idioms jostle helplessly one against another,
though he is possessed of a conviction that they could
be articulated one with another, if only he could find the
key. At this stage he cannot; and so all that is conveyed
is the desperation of the effort and the need. The language is a chronically unstable mix of linguistic elements from the European past, held together by will, by
nothing more than the urgency of the poet's need. Their
coherence is something wished for and vehemently ges-
tured at, certainly not demonstrated or achieved. The
vehemence of the need is quite without parallel among
poets writing and publishing in London in the first
decade of this century, and it is what at least one London reviewer of the time recognized and responded to.
This was Edward Thomas, himself still several years
short of working out the idiom which he commanded
under the stress of World War I for long enough to
make his own achievement in poetry irreplaceable. In
Pound's *Personae*, Thomas saw, as he said, a "battle-
field"; certainly not achievement, on the contrary the
debris of a defeat, but a defeat in which stronger forces
had been engaged than in any other engagement of a
living poet with the resources of the English tongue.
Pound's desperation, the ambitiousness or enormity of

what he was attempting, the scope of the conflict he provoked, the range of linguistic resources he challenged to battle—this was what Edwardian London, in the admittedly unrepresentative figure of Edward Thomas, responded to and recognized.[1] It is (to put it mildly) unlikely that London of the 1960s or 1970s would have responded with that generosity and percipience to a poet whose claim was, when all is said, almost wholly in promise rather than achievement. Pound was lucky to secure a firm reputation with the London elite on the score of *A Quinzaine for this Yule* (1908), and of *Personae* and *Exultations* (both 1909). Pound deserved the reputation; but in other periods reputations no less deserved have been withheld.

What Edward Thomas seems not to have recognized was that the peculiar rashness and impetuosity of the Edwardian poet he was responding to had everything to do with the fact that *this* Edwardian was American; that is to say, a poet of the English tongue to whom it came naturally to regard English as just one of the princely dialects of Europe.[2] An American like Pound came to *Europe*; and if he came to England, it was to one of the provinces of that larger cultural entity. No Edwardian Englishman thought of England that way; even if he was so intensely a Europeanist as Saintsbury,

[1] Edward Thomas, "Two Poets," *English Review*, Vol. 3 (1909), valuably excerpted in J. P. Sullivan, ed., *Ezra Pound*, Penguin Critical Anthology (1970) (hereinafter listed as "Sullivan: Penguin."). The full involvement of Thomas with early Pound is more extensive than had been realized, and it has yet to be studied; see items listed by Robert A. Corrigan, *Paideuma*, Vol. 1, no. 2 (1972), and Vol. 2, no. 1 (1973).
[2] I borrow this splendid phrase, without permission, from Donald Carne-Ross.

he defined himself in his national identity as that which
Continental Europe was not. But to a devoted American
Europeanist like the young Pound, what was precious
about England was not what marked her off from the
Continent but what bound her to the Mediterranean
heartlands. Hence the unconvincing impetuosity with
which the poet of "In Durance" moves from mock-
archaic English to Greek. Whitman before Pound had
interlarded his American English with tags of Spanish,
just as, after Pound, Wallace Stevens was to trick out
his American English with bits of French. But Pound's
endeavor was more serious altogether: he wanted to
create or re-create a *lingua franca* of Greco-Roman
Christendom in which English would operate as a sister
language with French and Spanish and Italian. The
mere *mix* of "In Durance" was to become the compound
language of *The Cantos*—a compound still perhaps unstable, but not so easily dissoluble.

The author of "In Durance" and of *The Spirit of
Romance* was the author also of *Patria Mia* (1912), in
which he wrote consciously and explicitly as a citizen of
the United States, addressing himself specifically to the
state of culture, and the prospects for culture, in his
native land. This curious brief work by Pound has had
an odd history, and was not published in book form
until more than thirty years after it was written, and
first appeared in A. R. Orage's London periodical, *The
New Age*. What is striking about it is that Pound the
American patriot is defeated almost before he starts; he
is trying to persuade himself that his native land is ripe
for a Renascence or a Risorgimento (he uses both terms,
as if they meant the same thing), and yet the evidence
belies him even as he assembles it. For he cannot bring

himself to acknowledge the implications of a paragraph on his second page:

> . . . the non-constructive idealist, the person who is content with his own thoughts, the person whom it is the fashion to call "sentimentalist," does not emigrate [Pound means, from Europe to the United States]. I mean the person who has "the finer feelings," love of home, love of land, love of place, of atmosphere, be he peasant or no. He may come as an act of heroism, but he returns to his land. He is almost negligible in our calculations.

Faced with the consequences of the Open Door policy on immigration, many relatively long-established American families, especially if they had come down in the world (and Pound's grandfather had been conspicuously richer and more notable than Pound's father was), shared, sixty years ago, this suspicion or conviction that Europe in the nineteenth century had unloaded on the United States only her more feckless and rootless and shallow-minded citizens. Because a significant proportion of those immigrants had been Jews from Eastern Europe, one product of this state of feeling was a distinctively American sort of anti-Semitism; and sure enough, anti-Jewish animus crops up in the original version of *Patria Mia*. In *Patria Mia*, Pound, sorting out his memories of going home for a long visit in 1910, oscillates between this annoyed snobbishness toward the recent immigrants and, on the other hand, a resentment at British condescension; he wants to believe that the United States is due to become a great cultural force in the world, and he tries to persuade himself of this, but in the end he fails. One must sympathize: it is hard for a man to acknowledge to himself at twenty-seven that he is always going to be happier outside his own country than in it. But the consequences were to be calamitous thirty years later, when Pound, still conceiving of himself as an American patriot, broadcast from Rome radio to the advancing American armies. And a particularly poignant twist emerges when Pound lists the things that the United States needed to do to bring her Renascence nearer: his recommendations are thoroughly American in that they are quite specific, and organizational, and practical. Most of them—for instance, massive endowments to the arts as well as to learning through charitable foundations, and the calculated provision for exchanges between scholars and practicing artists on university campuses—have, in fact, been implemented. Few Americans would want to assert, however, that these changes have brought about an artistic and cultural flowering in America, such as Pound tried to persuade himself was imminent in 1912.

It is in any case highly significant that this, Pound's most obviously and explicitly American book, should have a Latin title. He attempts to foresee a future for America according to paradigms he had learned about in Europe. Neither at this time nor afterward does Pound share the conviction and the hope which as a matter of historical record have fired the cultural achievements of the white man in North America ever since Plymouth Plantation—the hope and belief that the new continent offered a new start, a new Eden for a new Adam, liberated from the corruptions and errors of Europe and forewarned by European history of how to avoid European mistakes. On the contrary, Pound takes it for granted that if America is ever to produce or become a noble civilization, it can do so only by modeling itself on European precedents, precedents that are ultimately or originally Greek and Roman. In 1976 not many professors of Greek or Latin would make such sweeping claims for the worth of their studies. To one of them, Charles Doria, "trying to find the genesis and 'genius' of Western civilization through the classics" was the characteristic bent of classical studies for only a brief period—"from the 18th century until around the end of the first world war"; and throughout that period classical studies conducted in this style was serving some ugly ideological ends:

Greece and Italy become the discoverers and true cradles of our civilization. Classical writers, when read correctly, provided explanations for why Europe (and by extension America) grew to dominate the rest of the world. Democracy and Technology, the "gifts" of Athens and Rome respectively, can be traced back to the institutions and attitudes of the Ancients. Without them such modern touch-stones as progress, liberalism, individualism and "liberty under the law"—but above all the enlightened use of political and economic power for the good of the state (as taught in the Melian Dialogue of Thucydides) would have been philosophically impossible.

This relatively modern attitude of cultural autarky for Europe, of demonstrating her cultural and racial supremacy at the expense of everyone else, can best be described as the conversion of Classical Studies into Aryan Studies. It is no accident that throughout this period—. . . "from Winckelmann to Wilamowitz"

—Germany was the acknowledged leader in the scholarship of Antiquity.[3]

Obviously this account is as sweeping and schematic as the set of assumptions it sets out to discredit. But it is certainly instructive to see what Pound looks like from this standpoint. According to Doria, Pound, schooled in this way of thinking, "never got to the point . . . of seeing that Europe was not necessarily the daughter of Antiquity. . . . Pound made himself into a self-confident European who sums up in his poetry and criticism the contradictions and scattered beauties of that brutal civilization—possibly because he grew up at a time when that brutality was neither displayed openly nor recognized internally."[4] This is to see Pound as a desperate rear guard with a set of preconceptions that were superannuated almost as soon as he came to hold them. Thus it is near to the sense we have of him when we call him "Edwardian." And yet why on this showing is it always the professional classicists who assail him most brutally? There is a puzzle here, which we must grapple with in due course.

Yet this is far from being the view of Pound that prevails at the present day. One prevalent alternative view we have encountered already. It merges him, implausibly, with William Blake. But this too is a latecome image: one need not have lived to any advanced age to remember when Americans furiously denounced Pound as not American at all. Had he not lived all his

[3] Charles Doria, "Pound, Olson, and the Classical Tradition," in *Charles Olson: Essays, Reminiscences, Reviews*, Matthew Corrigan, ed., *Boundary*, Vol. 2, nos. 1 and 2 (State University of New York at Binghamton, 1973–74).
[4] *Ibid.*

adult years outside America? Was he not a notorious Fascist and anti-Semite? Had he not escaped conviction for treason on the trumped-up pretext of being unfit to plead? Memories are short; and now it is as if this climate of opinion had never been. In the interim the American literary intellectual, relieved of the embarrassment of Pound's incarceration in a Washington mental hospital, has found it possible to extol him as a great American poet—in contexts where "American" means emphatically "non-European." In these contexts the name that matters is not Blake but (inevitably) Whitman:

> . . . our sense of the vital relationship between Whitman and Pound . . . is indispensable to an understanding of the theory and history of American poetry. . . .[5]

Or again:

> The line from Whitman to Pound is the radical tradition of American poetry: the connection between them is quite as firm and unassailable as the *traditio* from Chaucer to Spenser to Milton. . . .[6]

"Firm and unassailable"—if this sounds like someone shouting down objections before they are raised, there is reason for it. For in *Patria Mia* what Pound wrote was:

> America of today is the sort of country that loses Henry James and retains to its appreciative bosom a certain Henry Van Dyke.

[5] Edwin Fussell, *Lucifer in Harness: American Meter, Metaphor, and Diction* (Princeton, 1973), pp. 20–21.
[6] *Ibid.* Even "What I feel about Walt Whitman" (1909) *American Literature*, xxvii, 1955, the one place where Pound is enthusiastic about Whitman, is much more ambiguous about him than Fussell's quotation from it would suggest.

The statement is a little drastic, but it has the facts behind it.

America's position in the world of art and letters is, relatively, about that which Spain held in the time of the Senecas. So far as civilization is concerned America is the great rich, Western province which has sent one or two notable artists to the Eastern capital. And that capital is, needless to say, not Rome, but the double city of London and Paris.

From our purely colonial conditions came Irving and Hawthorne. There [? Their] tradition was English unalloyed, and we had to ourselves Whitman, "The Reflex," who left us a human document, for you cannot call a man an artist until he shows himself capable of reticence and of restraint, until he shows himself in some degree master of the forces which beat upon him.

And in our own time the country has given to the world two men, Whistler, of the school of master-work, of the world of Dürer, and of Hokusai, and of Velazquez, and Mr. Henry James, in the school of Flaubert and Turgenev.

This passage has to mean that Whistler and James are superior to Whitman; that they are artists whereas Whitman is only "a reflex." Edwin Fussell quotes another passage of *Patria Mia* where Whitman is called "not an artist, but a reflex, the first honest reflex in an age of papier-mâché letters," and he comments: "Pound calls Whitman a 'reflex' and himself, by implication, another. . . ." But the inference is unwarranted: on the contrary, all the evidence suggests that Pound was vowing himself to be, not a "reflex" like Whitman, but an "artist" like James or Whistler. It was not thus that Milton looked back on Spenser, nor Spenser on Chaucer.

And at a time when a defaulting President of the United States has lately been forced from office by procedures laid down in the Constitution, the least one can say is that the question is still open whether the United States—its polity (in this case vindicated) framed on neoclassical models by assiduous Grecians like Jefferson and Adams—is not indeed, as Pound supposed, a last colony of the Greco-Roman world.

Meanwhile, though Pound's verse style is still radically insecure—in due course Allen Upward shall explain this for us, defining it as, in all its varieties, "Babu English"—Pound nonetheless had begun mapping what was to be his imaginative universe. And "mapping" is not altogether a metaphor: the most straightforward, and not the least reliable, way of apprehending Pound's universe is by recognizing the half-dozen geographical areas that are for him, and are to remain, "sacred places."[7] One of these, one of the most important, is already fixed upon and celebrated in the early poems. It is Lake Garda, haunt of Catullus and the scene, years later in Pound's life, of his momentous meeting with Joyce:

> *What hast thou, O my soul, with paradise?*
> *Will we not rather, when our freedom's won,*
> *Get us to some clear place wherein the sun*
> *Let's drift in on us through the olive leaves*
> *A liquid glory? If at Sirmio,*
> *My soul, I meet thee, when this life's outrun,*
> *Will we not find some headland consecrated*

[7] For another of the "sacred places" see Davie, "*The Cantos*: Towards a Pedestrian Reading," *Paideuma*, Vol. 1, no. 1 (1972).

> *By aery apostles of terrene delight,*
> *Will not our cult be founded on the waves,*
> *Clear sapphire, cobalt, cyanine,*
> *On triune azures, the impalpable*
> *Mirrors unstill of the eternal change?*
>
> *Soul, if She meet us there, will any rumour*
> *Of havens more high and courts desirable*
> *Lure us beyond the cloudy peak of Riva?*
>
> (FROM CANZONI, 1911)

This is far from being the only place in the early collections where Pound's style achieves a temporary and trembling synthesis, and a sort of limpid eagerness that is very attractive indeed. In another early poem, for instance, "The Flame," he used the Latin name for Lake Garda, "Benacus," to come up with the astonishing lines:

> *Sapphire Benacus, in thy mists and thee*
> *Nature herself's turned metaphysical.*
> *Who can look on that blue and not believe?*

It will be noted that these verses have none of the characteristics that we are likely to think of as "modern," any more than the verses which Thomas Hardy, because of the same Catullan associations, had devoted to the same spot only a few years before.[8]

[8] See "Catullus: XXXI. (After passing Sirmione, April 1887)," *The Collected Poems of Thomas Hardy* (London, 1952), p. 166.

●●
11

William Carlos Williams, along with "H.D." (Hilda Doolittle), had been the most valuable literary acquaintance that Pound had made at the University of Pennsylvania. In 1918, in the Prologue to his *Kora in Hell* (1920), Williams wrote of Eliot's "La Figlia Che Piange": "It is the latest touch from the literary cuisine, it adds to the pleasant outlook from the club window. If to do this, if to be a Whistler at best, in the art of poetry, is to reach the height of poetic expression then Ezra and Eliot have approached it and *tant pis* for the rest of us." This is unfair to Eliot, though it is hard to say just how, since Williams' rancor is so unfocused. It is unfair to Pound too; yet Pound had invited it, having trailed his coat about Whistler so often.

We can hardly believe that Pound's admira-

tion for Whistler's painting was not dashed a little as
soon as he began, about 1910, consorting with Wyndham Lewis. But one may suspect, in any case, that
Pound responded less to what Whistler did when he
confronted a canvas than to what he did when he faced
a London drawing room. Pound, it seems clear, was
acutely conscious of his situation as an American artist
in London, and of the sheerly social embarrassments
and uncertainties which that let him in for. For what
he felt as his disabling "colonialism," or for the dis-
qualifications of that sort which he imagined his British
associates imputing to him, he overcompensated with
aggressive affectations of dress and behavior, a calculated outrageousness which he seems to have concocted
on Whistler's model. The trick of it was to maintain a
running allusion to a largely fictitious Paris; for if, as
Pound had said in *Patria Mia*, the cultural capital for
the American was the twin-city of Paris/London, one
anticipated and pre-empted any charge of provincialism
by a hint that London might be provincial by compari-
son with Paris. In Whistler's day, when Henri Murger's
Scènes de la Vie de Bohème was still a recent book, the
device worked very well; when Pound thirty years later
cultivated the same or similar mannerisms, they were a
shabbier disguise, and keen and compassionate eyes
could penetrate them to the eager insecurity behind.[1]

Pound met Eliot in 1914. And Eliot's strategy, as
every one knows, was very different. It was protective
coloration; he became *plus anglais que les anglais*. Not
a hint of Whistler in *his* demeanor! And in the long run

[1] See Herbert Read in 1918, as cited by W. K. Rose, "Pound
and Lewis: The Crucial Years," *Agenda*, Vol. 7, no. 3.—Vol.
8, no. 1 (1969–70) (*Wyndham Lewis Special Issue*): 130.

it may seem that Eliot's strategy served him better; it moved him smoothly into the columns of *The Athenaeum* and the *Times Literary Supplement*, into the circles of Bloomsbury, into partnership in an influential publishing house, ultimately to the Order of Merit and a memorial in Westminster Abbey. But this will seem a success story only to those for whom the prizes worth having are dispensed by the British. And if Pound ever thought this, certainly from 1920 onward he thought otherwise; he thought that Eliot had compromised himself more than he intended and more than was good for him or his talent; and so in the *really* long run Pound was sure that his was the better strategy after all. It worked better in the short term—yet for no very creditable reason. For by 1910 or 1914 bohemianism was what English bourgeois society expected of its artists; as long as the self-styled artists indulged in bohemian antics, the solid citizen knew where he stood with them, and could extend an amused tolerance. Their manifestoes and exhibitions were part of the London scene; part of what Tommy Atkins came home to on leave, if he was so inclined; they were among the home fires that were kept burning. This was on the assumption that they had nothing to do with, and nothing to say about, the grotesque horrors across the Channel which Tommy came on leave from, and returned to. When that assumption was challenged, and the dishonorable terms of that tolerant compact rejected, the challenge and the rejection came not from Pound or Eliot or Wyndham Lewis but from a second-rate poet, the stiffly Anglo-Jewish gentleman Siegfried Sassoon. Meanwhile, as long as Pound sustained the vehemently and inventively amusing bohemian front, and Eliot behind him perfected his Anglicized camouflage, the Eliot-Pound tandem worked very effectively indeed—especially for Eliot![2]

But Pound was front-runner and fairground barker for many besides Eliot, in those years before and during World War I. One of the things that Paris exported to London (and thence to Chicago, if a London-based American like Pound had anything to do with it) was "movements." In 1914, run-of-the-mill critics could still juggle decorously, and sometimes to some purpose, with the timeworn counters: romanticism, classicism, realism. There had also been "naturalism," a sort of realism carried to excess under the patent of Emile Zola, on which suitably temperate and level-headed things had been said by Sir Edmund Gosse; there had been "symbolism," associated chiefly with the name of Paul Verlaine, on which Arthur Symons had written definitively in *The Symbolist Movement in Literature* (1899); and there had been "impressionism," a term carried over from French painting into English poetry by the same Arthur Symons, in whose poems it seemed to have to do chiefly with sad prostitutes sheltering in London doorways from the London rain. All in all, London in 1910— unlike the London of Mr. Podsnap, on which Whistler had impinged—thought it was open-minded about innovations from the Continent and had shown itself able to acclimatize them. Was not George Gissing, were not the young H. G. Wells and Arnold Bennett entirely presentable naturalists? Had not the young W. B. Yeats, in *The Wind among the Reeds* and *The Wanderings of*

[2] It must be said, however, that during this period Eliot's *private* life, after his marriage in 1915, was very unhappy, indeed agonizing.

Oisin, mastered the calculated vagueness that was thought to be the central device of Stéphane Mallarmé's symbolism? And was not the young Ford Madox Hueffer (Ford) an impressionist in a rather less restricted and more significant sense than Arthur Symons? London was conscious of having broken out of insularity, of being much less provincial than it had been, and it was accordingly benign to young turks like Pound and Wyndham Lewis, be they never so American.

Now there came talk of "unanimism," of "post-impressionism," "fauvism," even (this one from Italy) "futurism." The London intelligentsia expected people like Pound and Lewis to keep it abreast of these novelties. And Pound embraced the role with relish, helping to provide London with two homegrown movements of its own: "Imagism" and "Vorticism." (Another such, "Georgianism," launched by Edward Marsh in 1912 and embodied in five anthologies of *Georgian Poetry* appearing between then and 1922, reached a much wider public than either imagism or vorticism.)

Both these last were serious movements, and their force is not yet spent. Unfortunately, in both cases the seriousness escapes all but the most attentive and sympathetic students, because of the publicity stunts and bohemian high jinks with which Pound promoted them. And yet "promotion" is of the nature of any artistic movement. From one point of view any such movement is a social phenomenon, navigating in the light and fitful winds of fashion to provide new catchphrases and talking points for each new publishing season. And at the same time it emerges out of a jostling for the limelight among competing cliques of young artists, each group marketing a product that it tries to make more distinctive and more intriguing than the wares of its competitors. Not just Eliot and Lewis but Robert Frost and H. D. and Marianne Moore, most of all Joyce, had reason over the years to be grateful to Pound for the energy, the zest, and the hard-headedness behind the calculated flamboyance with which he grabbed the limelight on their behalf.

Imagism (originally "imagisme," as if by French spelling to borrow the required Parisian *éclat*) was an exclusively literary movement, whereas the later vorticism claimed to comprehend all the arts and was strongest in painting and sculpture. Yet Pound himself seems to have thought of vorticism as only a prolongation and theoretical elaboration of what he had fought for under the banner of imagism, until imagism was taken away from him, and trivialized, by Amy Lowell.[3] If we ask for the theory of imagism, it is otherwise hard to find; though it can be put together out of certain speculations of T. E. Hulme as early as 1909, at which time the movement had had a sort of aborted birth. But the imagism of 1913, when Pound's energy and impudence made it a talking point in London and Chicago, was not theoretical at all but came across as two or three punchily expressed rules of thumb, as in the famous "A Few Don'ts for an Imagist":

Use no superfluous word, no adjective, which does not reveal something.

Don't use such an expression as "dim lands of *peace*." It dulls the image. It mixes an abstraction with the concrete. It comes from the writer's not

[3] The history of imagism has been written several times, and the earliest such history is still the best: Glenn Hughes, *Imagism and the Imagists* (Stanford, 1931).

realizing that the natural object is always the *adequate* symbol.

Go in fear of abstractions. Don't retell in mediocre verse what has already been done in good prose. Don't think any intelligent person is going to be deceived when you try to shirk all the difficulties of the unspeakably difficult art of good prose by chopping your composition into line lengths. . . .

Don't imagine that the art of poetry is any simpler than the art of music, or that you can please the expert before you have spent at least as much effort on the art of verse as the average piano teacher spends on the art of music.

Be influenced by as many great artists as you can, but have the decency either to acknowledge the debt outright, or to try to conceal it.

Don't allow "influence" to mean merely that you mop up the particular decorative vocabulary of some one or two poets whom you happen to admire. . . .

Use either no ornament or good ornament.[4]

This is a striking change from the "Romance language" of only a few months before. And with pronouncements in this impatient plain-man idiom there emerged the figure of Pound the iconoclast, a rhetorical illusion which still too often obscures the lineaments of the man who fabricated and deployed the rhetoric for certain short-term purposes; who chose for those temporary purposes to conceal the far from "plain-man" perspectives that he nonetheless had in mind. In the case of imagism, for instance, if no body of theory

[4] Pound's "A Few Don'ts for an Imagist," originally part of an article, "Imagisme," written in collaboration with F. S. Flint for *Poetry* in 1913, was reprinted with alterations in "A Retrospect," *Literary Essays* (1954). The version I give is from Sullivan: Penguin.

underpinned the pithy categorical directives, on the other hand, there lay behind them a reading of literary history. This Pound had derived from Ford Madox Ford —to whom accordingly he always wanted to give more credit than to Hulme. When Pound during his first years in London had gone for instruction to Yeats at one time of day and to Ford at another, what he learned from Ford was that for more than a century the strongest and most devoted literary imaginations had by and large applied themselves to writing novels rather than poems; accordingly, that one field of experience after another (which is to say, one range of language after another) had been lost to poetry and become a province of prose fiction; and so, if poetry were to recover anything like the centrality and dignity it once had, poets must wrest back some of the lost provinces by beating the novelists at their own game, by using language in the same way as the great novelists, with at least equal clarity, force, and precision. Others since Ford have perceived just such a deflection of imaginative energy from the poem into the novel in the nineteenth century; but what was striking about Ford's contention was that the novelist he had in mind was not a Dickens or a Herman Melville, whose cast of mind can readily be recognized as in some obvious sense "poetic," but rather the great French masters, and of these not Balzac, but Stendhal and Flaubert, together with, as a sort of honorary Frenchman, Turgenev. And this was more than Francophile snobbery on Ford's part; for by his argument the qualities of language which the poet had to recover by emulating novelists were the virtues of prose at its most prosaic—exactness above all, *le mot juste*. In Pound's mind imagism was, perhaps centrally, a program for bringing into poetry the Flaubertian *mot juste*. In other words, it was, despite appearances, just one more program in, or out of, "Romance languages."

Nor must it be thought that the mind of the young American was a *tabula rasa* on which Ford imprinted his European aphorisms and prejudices. From the Martial and Catullus and Horace that Pound had read before leaving America, as from Bertrand de Born and Villon and pre-eminently from Dante himself, Pound was well aware of ranges of language (hence, of human experience) that had once been available to the poet, and which appeared to be available no longer, unless the poet should exert himself to retrieve them. Odd as it may seem, even the example of his other mentor, Yeats (who was, he declared, the magnet that drew him to England in the first place), impelled him in the same direction. One thing he admired in *The Wind among the Reeds* was prosaically normal word order within the sentence; and sure enough, that had been one avowed intention of The Rhymers' Club with which Yeats had associated himself in the 1890s.

The *mot juste* that Ford and Pound admired was to be found as readily in Catullus or Villon or indeed George Crabbe as in Flaubert. And a Catullus or a Villon was more instructive than Flaubert because, like any poet of any century, each had had to deny himself the cumulative effect with which a Flaubert could re-create a whole milieu by a multitude of exactly registered particulars. Upon the poet there was imposed the further task of selecting, from among the array of significant‚ particulars, that one, or those one or two, which could be made, by judicious deployment of a specifically poetic resource like cadence, to stand for all the rest. And so there enters into Pound's thinking the principle of "the luminous detail," the single particular which, chosen with enough care and rendered with enough exactness, can impel the reader to summon up for himself all the other particulars implied by that salient one. It is a principle crucial to all poetic structures, as Pound realized, finding it corroborated by the Chinese poetry that he had toyed with already in the pages of Herbert Allen Giles[5] and that he encountered more intimately in the drafts made by Ernest Fenollosa out of which he fashioned the beautiful translations of *Cathay* (1915). In later life Pound was to suppose, perilously, that this principle which worked for poetic structures applied to intellectual structures also, so that, for instance, the entire thought of Saint Ambrose could be deduced from the animated pondering of one luminous page of his writings.[6]

Pound was in trouble, in any case. For the valuable prosaicism which Ford had taught him to look for and demand is much more readily attainable, perhaps also more important, in poetry written for the speaking voice than in poetry that aspires to be sung. And yet Pound's natural bent and talent had always been for poetry that should be sung, rather than for such spoken *genres* as epigram, lampoon, epistle. Apart from anything else, these *genres* call for a sure grasp of social tone, whereas there is much evidence that Pound was socially maladroit.[7] Accordingly, in the years of imagism and vorticism we

[5] The versions from the Chinese in *Lustra* (1916) were derived from Giles's *Chinese Poetry in English Verse* (1884) or else his *History of Chinese Literature* (1901).
[6] See Noel Stock, *Reading the Cantos: A Study of Meaning in Ezra Pound* (New York, 1967), pp. 106–107.
[7] See W. K. Rose, *loc. cit.*, p. 124. And compare Robert Mc-

find him painstakingly attempting, in epigram and lampoon, niceties of urbane insolence and Jamesian nuance such as he could not command. (In any case he was by nature genial and good-humored.) His most elaborate endeavor of this kind was to be *Hugh Selwyn Mauberley* (1920), but many of his shorter pieces of 1914 and 1915, as collected in *Lustra* (1916), are meant to be urbane and poised but succeed only in being *arch*. And in *Cathay* what we cherish is not "The Jewel Stairs' Grievance," excitedly footnoted by Pound to show how it alludes to points of social decorum, but "Song of the Bowmen of Shu," which was remembered by poor Henri Gaudier-Brzeska when he wrote from the trenches.[8]

In these straits the ancient master who served Pound best was Catullus, in those of his epigrams which were at the furthest remove from the sardonic harshness of Martial; with these for a model Pound could achieve the chiseled dryness of the *mot juste* while reaching back, as Catullus had done, to the plangency of the Greek epigram. Peter Whigham, who has made confessedly Poundian versions of Catullus, detects Catullus as a model in Pound's poems of this period where we should not, unaided, recognize either Catullus or epigram. Such is the very winning poem of 1915, "The Gypsy," which Whigham thinks is near to Catullus XLVI.[9] This allows us to scotch a possible misconception: for the sentiment

---

Almon, *Being Geniuses Together 1920–1930*, Kay Boyle, ed. (New York, 1968), p. 100.

[8] Letter of December 27, 1914, to John Cournos. See Robert A. Corrigan, *Paideuma*, Vol. 1, no. 2 (1972): 251.

[9] I have discussed "The Gypsy," along with Wordsworth's "Stepping Westwards," in my *Articulate Energy: An Inquiry into the Syntax of English Poetry* (New York, 1955).

of "The Gypsy" is in a fairly obvious sense "romantic."
But then so is the Catullus poem insofar as it turns on
"lust of travel" (in Whigham's translation). And so
there is no question of making Pound out to be "classical" or a "classicist," as against "romantic" or "roman-
ticist." What I have suggested is that Pound was,
despite appearances, *conservative*; and to be conservative in his generation meant prolonging some romantic
attitudes as well as prolonging or reviving preromantic
ones.

We are in much the same case with another of
Pound's enthusiasms—for Jules Laforgue, whose prece-
dent was as important for Pound as for Eliot. It is not to
the point to observe that Laforgue's irony and his wit
ride on top of romantic melancholy, that they are distinctively post-Byronic and light-years away from the
preromantic robustness of Ben Jonson. Laforgue knew
this better than anyone, and much of his wit turns upon
his recognizing the anomaly in himself. It is his doing
so which commends him to both Eliot and Pound. The
latter, though he admired the caustic severity of Martial
and Jonson, was never able to equal it, and didn't often
try.[10]

Arthur Symons had declared Laforgue a symbolist,
and Tristan Corbière along with him. But Pound's sense
of his French predecessors had far less to do with
Symons' *Symbolist Movement in Literature* than had
Yeats's or (at least initially) Eliot's. Laforgue and

[10] I have in mind here Yvor Winters' remarks on Laforgue in
"The Experimental School in American Poetry" (1937), reprinted in *In Defense of Reason* (Denver, 1947), and in
Discussions of Poetry: Form and Structure, F. E. X. Murphy,
ed. (New York, 1964), pp. 39–43.

Corbière he admired, but for aspects of their work which had nothing to do with *symbolisme*. Similarly he admired Arthur Rimbaud, but the young Rimbaud who wrote "Les Chercheuses de Poux," not Rimbaud the *voyant*. It is hardly too much to say that what Pound admired in these Frenchmen was what he admired also in Crabbe—the naming of quotidian or ignoble objects with an accuracy that depended on purging from the mind any sense of the associations that had accrued to them. Just that purged accuracy was what constituted *le mot juste*, whether in verse or prose. And what Pound was looking for becomes clear when we add to these French names another, Théophile Gautier, whom no one has called a *symboliste*. For Pound, Gautier was the greatest French master of them all because, along with the Crabbesque virtues, he had, quite consciously and programmatically, just what Crabbe so disastrously lacked—a sense for the sculptural: "*Sculpte, lime, cisèle....*" And in this way Pound could come full circle to the epigram of the ancient world; in Greek, the very word "epigram" embodies the analogy that Gautier insisted on, which Pound was to cherish henceforth, demanding from poetry "hardness" and "cut"—the analogy, that is, between words on the page or given to the air, and letters or other shapes incised upon a stone slab.

It follows that Pound had little patience with the central endeavor of *symbolisme*, which explored the analogy not with sculpture but with music. It is easy to get this wrong. Have I not just insisted that Pound wanted to write poems for singing rather more than poems for speaking? And do we not find him at every possible opportunity telling poets how much a study of music

will do for them? Yes; but the music that Pound has in
mind is real sounds in sequence, an actual melody,
whereas the idea of music which fascinated Mallarmé
and Valéry was precisely that—the *idea* of music, the
idea of a poetic art that should be nonreferential or
self-referential like the art of music. Pound seemingly
had no interest in that. What Pound had in mind was
a marriage of the two arts, not an analogy between
them; not one of them transformed so as to "approach
the condition" of the other but each in its distinctness
collaborating with and enriching the other. (Eliot in his
1917 essay, *Ezra Pound: His Metric and Poetry*, says
otherwise but, I think, wrongly.) And so it still needs
to be stressed that the momentousness of imagism as
Pound conceived of it lies just in its being not a variant
of *symbolisme* or a development out of it, but a radical
alternative to it. This is clear from Pound's occasional
writings, such as his 1914 review of Yeats's *The Green
Helmet*. But it is a point made most explicitly, appropriately enough, in a tribute to a sculptor, Gaudier-Brzeska,
killed in the Flanders trenches. Yet *Gaudier-Brzeska: A
Memoir* (1916) is overtly concerned with vorticism, not
imagism—which only shows how the two movements
were, in Pound's sense of the matter, really one. *Gaudier-
Brzeska* is a work of theory; and so the difference between *symbolisme* and imagism can there be presented
as philosophical, epistemological. It should not by this
time surprise us that in this perspective imagism is
revealed as the conservative and traditional rejoinder to
symbolisme's dangerous innovations. The traditional authority that Pound appeals to is Aquinas. Like Aquinas,
the imagist holds that a proposition—for instance, "the
pine tree in mist upon the far hill looks like a fragment

of Japanese armor"—is either true or false; true or false, not just to the state of mind or angle of vision of the perceiver but to the real appearance, the real relations in real space, of what is perceived. Either what is reported of pine trees and plates of armor is a true account of the spatial and other relations asserted, or else it is not true, however honestly it may reproduce the impression produced upon a perceiver who may be abnormally situated or in an abnormal state of mind. The idea of "normality" is unphilosophical, in the sense that one takes on faith the existence of a norm in perceiving. But the imagist will make that act of faith, just as common sense does, and as the *symboliste* does not. Pound, like Gautier, is one of those *"pour qui le monde visible existe"*; and the best pages of *Gaudier-Brzeska* are those in which Pound most exultantly justifies that proclivity, and insists on the impoverishment that comes as soon as we begin to doubt that the perceivable world truly exists as something other than ourselves, bodied against us. On the other hand, we must not suppose that our organs of perception are limited to the five senses; Pound was sure—for some of us, excessively sure—that they were not. (It is worth remarking that Eliot, the student of F. H. Bradley and author of "The Love Song of J. Alfred Prufrock," would have had to take the *symboliste* side in this quarrel; but it looks as if neither Pound nor Eliot chose to bring this to a head.)

As for the more abstruse reaches of Pound's argument, those which have to do with the central concept of "the vortex," they rest upon the formulations of a British thinker, man of letters, and publicist named Allen Upward, whom Pound had met in 1911, and who already in 1908 had been appealing to the authority of

Confucius and Mencius. We are not yet in a position to establish even the bare facts of Upward's life, let alone to define the full scope and tenor of his thought,[11] though Pound never ceased, even in the last verses he published, to cry out on this as a scandal. Upward remains sunk in oblivion, though one has only to read chapters thirteen and fourteen of his *The New Word* (1908) to recognize a powerful and original mind clearly and trenchantly concerned with matters that bear directly on what Pound meant by "vortex." It was a case like this, of the unconventional thinker effectively gagged by simple or deliberate neglect and indifference, which in later years converted Pound to a conspiracy theory of history, in which the worst, most murderous conspiracies were conspiracies of silence. Wyndham Lewis, though in one sense the whole vorticist program had been devised for his benefit, declared that he didn't understand what "vorticism" meant.[12] Pound understood; and if we don't, it is because we haven't looked where he told us to.

[11] Bryant Knox, "Allen Upward and Ezra Pound," *Paideuma*, Vol. 3, no. 1 (1974), has however made a start.
[12] Cf. Lewis in one of his last letters: "Vorticism. This name is an invention of Ezra Pound. . . . What does this word mean? I do not know." (Quoted by W. K. Rose, *loc. cit.*, p. 125.)

Hugh Selwyn Mauberley
and
Homage to Sextus Propertius

Anecdotes by Wyndham Lewis and others give us one coherent and believable picture of Pound in his London years—mannered, driving, and (his own word as applied to Browning) "rambunctious." Some letters that he wrote to Thomas Hardy present a different picture, in some ways more attractive. One of them seems to have been written in February 1921:

> My Dear Thomas Hardy,
> Of course your last note does not, did not require any answer—any more than my rather bold envoi of books needed acknowledgment —only it is so exceedingly difficult to get any criticism whatever from anyone whose reactions one respects—there is the malice engendered by stupidity—and the hurried hackwork of poor devils who have to write reviews—that

if you have by any chance looked at the wretched
brochures again and found any specific merit or de-
merit, it would be no inconsiderable kindness to send
me word—not a politeness. The Propertius is con-
fused—the Mauberley is thin—one tries to comfort
oneself with the argument that the qualities are in-
herent in the subject matter. . . .

. . . I don't think mere praise is any good—I know
where I can get it, and just what *wrong* reasons
would lead one or two eminent contemporaries to like
or tolerate certain passages.

Forgive me if I blurt out this demand for more
frankness than anything, save perhaps a lifelong
friendship, can engender between two individuals.

Sincerely,
Ezra Pound[1]

Pound and Hardy never met; and Hardy was so elab-
orately cagey and positively misleading with interview-
ers that the encounter which never took place need not
be much regretted. Yet there are some painfully self-
accusing pages of *Guide to Kulchur* (1938) which show
that Hardy's personality and poems were of absorbing
interest to Pound, and it is easy to see why.[2] To begin
with, since Pound had convinced himself that the poets
must meet and beat the nineteenth-century novelists on
their own terms, what spectacle could be more compelling than that of Hardy, who, having achieved fame
as a Victorian novelist, after *Jude the Obscure* wrote
only poems up to his death in 1928? Moreover, Hardy
translated Catullus and, as Pound did not fail to note

---

[1] Patricia Hutchins, "Ezra Pound and Thomas Hardy,"
Southern Review (Winter 1968).
[2] See particularly chapter 52.

many years later, "no man ever had so much Latin and
so eschewed the least appearance of being a classicist
on the surface." Not just Latin, Greek also: "he translated a Sapphic fragment, labeling it 'imitation' to avoid
quibbling."[3] Hardy was at such pains to cover his
tracks, even going to the length of ghosting his own
biography, that no one can say for certain either that
he did or that he did not read Georges Duhamel's and
Charles Vildrac's *Notes sur la technique poétique*
(1911), as Pound certainly did.[4] In any case, by that
avenue or more probably some other, Hardy by 1912
had got to the point of imitating—not copying—Greek
meters; before Pound embarked on the same course,
Hardy had been using "falling rhythm (. . . dactylo-
trochaic) rather than the familiar English rising (or
iambic) rhythm," and had been making "a much more
extensive use than had been common in serious English
verse of trisyllabic feet."[5]

> *Woman much missed, how you call to me, call to me,*
> *Saying that now you are not as you were*
> *When you had changed from the one who was all to*
> *   me,*
> *But as at first, when our day was fair.*
>
> *Can it be you that I hear? Let me view you, then,*
> *Standing as when I drew near to the town*
> *Where you would wait for me: yes, as I knew you*
> *   then,*
> *Even to the original air-blue gown!*

[3] *Confucius to Cummings: An Anthology of Poetry*, Ezra
Pound and Marcella Spann, eds., p. 325.
[4] D. S. Carne-Ross, "New Metres for Old: A Note on Pound's
Metric," *Arion*, Vol. 6 (1967); in Sullivan: Penguin, pp.
347–49.
[5] *Ibid.*

This is from "The Voice," one of the *Poems of 1912–13* which, so Pound was to say, "lift him to his apex, sixteen poems from 'The Going' to 'Castle Boterel,' all good, and enough for a lifetime."[6] Moreover, Ford's *English Review*, which, as long as it lasted, was the journal most favored by both Pound and Lewis, had been started in 1908—so Ford said, and Pound repeated it—to get a Hardy poem into print. Altogether there were abundant reasons why Pound, sincerely and touchingly wanting in 1921 an impartial opinion of his most ambitious poems to that date, should have written out of the blue to Hardy rather than to any one else.

Hardy's reply is among the Pound papers in the Beineke Library at Yale. The substance of it can be deduced from the letter which it provoked from Pound, dated March 31, 1921:

Dear Thomas Hardy,

It is very good of you to answer—and though you seem to think you have said little or nothing, you have really said a great deal and diagnosed the trouble with nearly all art and literature of the past thirty years.

I ought—precisely—to have written "Propertius Soliloquizes"—turning the reader's attention to the reality of Propertius—but no—what I do is to borrow a term—aesthetic—a term of aesthetic *attitude* from a French musician, Debussy—who uses "Homage à Rameau" for a title to a piece of music recalling Rameau's manner. My "Homage" is not an English word at all.

There are plenty of excuses—and no justification. I come from an American suburb—where I was not born—where both parents are really foreigners, i.e.

6 *Confucius to Cummings, loc. cit.*

one from New York and one from Wisconsin. The
suburb has no roots, no centre of life. I imitate
Browning. At a tender age London critics scare me
out [of] frank and transparent imitation—even "Propertius Soliloquizes" would sound too much like one
of R.B.'s titles.

Result:—I fall into the error current since 1890.
I ought to have concentrated on the subject—(I did
so long as I forgot my existence for the sake of the
lines)—and I tack on a title relating to the treatment
—in a fit of nerves—fearing the reader won't suffi-
ciently see the super-position [?] the doubling of me
and Propertius, England to-day and Rome under
Augustus. . . .

The blurted out self-diagnosis of the third paragraph—
how extraordinary, to have New York declared foreign
to Philadelphia!—is exceptionally important, and we
shall return to it. On the narrower issue of what the
poem should have been called (that is to say, what
genre it belongs to), Pound surely concedes too much.
"Propertius Soliloquizes" would have made Pound's
poem into a Browningesque dramatic monologue, which
it certainly isn't; and it would not have helped the
reader to what Pound seems to think so important—"the
doubling of me and Propertius, England to-day and
Rome under Augustus." Yet this declared intention is
itself at odds with what the letter says elsewhere: "I
ought to have concentrated on the subject—(I did so
long as I forgot my existence for the sake of the
lines). . . ." For how could Pound be forgetting his own
existence, if at the same time he was trying to define
rather precisely his relation to the British Empire at a
specific historical moment in its decline? If that avowed

purpose had been his real one, there was a genre specifically fashioned to serve that purpose—the "imitation" in the strict sense, as in Pope's "Ode to Augustus" or Johnson's "Vanity of Human Wishes." And yet Pound's poem belongs in that genre even less than it belongs with Browning's dramatic monologues. I have come to suspect that the whole business about "the doubling of me and Propertius" is a rationalization after the fact, a fiction uneasily promoted by Pound to meet a parrot-cry for "contemporary relevance." The British imperial decline is not really *in* Pound's poem at all, though we can import it into our experience of the poem if we let ourselves be bluffed into doing so. A more rewarding experience of *Homage to Sextus Propertius* (1919) becomes possible if we think of the poet as forgetting his own existence "for the sake of the lines." And if that sounds like sacrificing "life" to "art," it is nothing of the kind, as we shall see.

In any case, Pound set great store by Hardy's criticism; not only does he reproduce the self-accusing substance of this letter in his tribute to Hardy in *Guide to Kulchur*, but in *The Pisan Cantos* he speaks of carrying Hardy's letter about with him as a sort of talisman, at all events as the single prize worth keeping from his London years. The point was, perhaps, that on top of the metrical and other interests they shared Hardy stood in very much the same relation to Browning as Pound did. "Hardy at his best," so Pound was to say, "stems out of Browning, as Ford does, and does so by shedding the encrustation."[7] And certainly, among the many late-

---

[7] *Ibid.*

Victorian voices that echo or whisper in Pound's earliest poems, Browning's voice is the loudest and clearest. Nor was that the end of Browning's importance; his *Sordello* was one of the earliest instigations to, and even models for, *The Cantos*, as the original first three Cantos, first published in 1919 and subsequently replaced, make very clear. The extent of this Browningesque influence at a technical level is something that has never yet been fully investigated;[8] but Browning is in any case the most Italophile of the Victorian poets, with the possible exception of his friend Landor, and so he would have appealed to Pound anyway. The historic Sordello, a Provençal poet of Mantua strikingly commemorated by Dante, was inevitably a hero for Pound as for Browning. And in *Lustra*, there had appeared "Near Perigord," a poem of capital importance which boiled down into less than two hundred lines the central concern of Browning's *The Ring and the Book*—that is to say, the seeking for historical truth through the conflicting testimonies of interested witnesses.

"Boiling down," indeed, was very much Pound's concern at this period, as we see elsewhere in the second letter to Hardy, when he writes of the other poem he had sent:

> If—as in the case of Mauberley's own amorous adventure, I compress Henry James' novel into two pages—even unsuccessfully—I have the right to some of the attention that would have gone to the 298 pages omitted.

[8] But see Jacob Korg, "The Music of Lost Dynasties: Browning, Pound and History," *ELH, A Journal of English Literary History*, Vol. 39, no. 3 (1972).

But about this poem, *Hugh Selwyn Mauberley*, it is best to be brief.[9] This poem is, and has proved to be, the most accessible of Pound's longer poems, the one that it is easiest to start with. For just that reason it is a poem that one must grow through, and grow out of, though the literary world is full of people who got this far and no further—for whom, accordingly, this is Pound's best poem, or the only one of his poems that is "an assured achievement." Pound's word for it, when he sent it to Hardy, was "thin"—"the Mauberley is thin." And "thin" may well be the right word, which explains why thin and constricted and rancorously distrustful sensibilities can respond to this poem by Pound as to no other.

Hugh Selwyn Mauberley consists of two sequences, one of thirteen poems dated 1919, followed by one of five poems dated 1920. The appearance of intricate interlinkings and cross references between the sequences and between the poems is, I now think, largely illusory. But one that is not an illusion is the relationship between the poem that closes the second sequence, "Medallion," and the poem that closes the first, "Envoi." It has been proved[10] that these two poems are companion pieces; that they have the same subject, the singing of Raymonde Collignon, whose London recitals Pound reported (mostly under a pseudonym) when he was music critic for *The New Age*. Raymonde Collignon en-

---

[9] Many commentaries are available, including two I have written myself, the first of which I now want to disown. See Davie, "Ezra Pound's 'Hugh Selwyn Mauberley'," *The Modern Age. Pelican Guide to English Literature* (London, 1961), pp. 315–29; and Davie, *Ezra Pound: Poet as Sculptor*, pp. 91–101.
[10] By Jo Brantley Berryman, *Paideuma*, Vol. 2, no. 3 (1973).

deared herself to Pound in any case, by singing Provençal poems to the Provençal melodies which Pound had assisted Walter Morse Rummel to recover, back in 1911.[11] But in "Envoi," at any rate, she is singing songs of a later date, from the English seventeenth century:

Go, dumb-born book,
Tell her that sang me once that song of Lawes:
Hadst thou but song
As thou hast subjects known,
Then were there cause in thee that should condone
Even my faults that heavy upon me lie,
And build her glories their longevity.

Tell her that sheds
Such treasure in the air,
Recking naught else but that her graces give
Life to the moment,
I would bid them live
As roses might, in magic amber laid,
Red overwrought with orange and all made
One substance and one colour
Braving time.

Tell her that goes
With song upon her lips
But sings not out the song, nor knows
The maker of it, some other mouth,
May be as fair as hers,
Might, in new ages, gain her worshippers,
When our two dusts with Waller's shall be laid,
Siftings on siftings in oblivion,
Till change hath broken down
All things save Beauty alone.

[11] See Walter Morse Rummel, *Hesternae Rosae, Serta II* (London, 1913).

This is *modern* verse? Wherein is it modern? In meter? In diction? In sentiment? Is it, for instance, in any of these respects distinctively an American poem rather than an English one? Ah no; but it *is* distinctively American all the same. For Thomas E. Connolly[12] was surely right to identify the "her" of the third stanza with England or the English poetic tradition, perhaps the English "muse," certainly the English language; and hence to take "some other mouth" to mean some non-English mouth which nonetheless speaks English—that is to say, an American mouth. After all, when *Hugh Selwyn Mauberley* first appeared in an American edition, the title page carried a note which read: "The sequence is so distinctly a farewell to London that the reader who chooses to regard this as an exclusively American edition may as well omit it. . . ." English readers should have been ashamed and distressed by this contention—this triumphant demonstration—that the English lyric tradition was thenceforth in American hands, British hands having proved too limp for the task. And in *Antheil and the Treatise on Harmony* (1924) Pound was to drive the point home:

There is no copy of Henry Lawes' three volumes of "Ayres and Dialogues" at the little second-hand music shop in Great Turnestyle, but the kindly proprietor is good enough to look up old sale catalogues. The last set went for £49. Dolmetsch' arrangements of some of this old music are out of print. Only in a nation utterly contemptuous of its past treasures and inspired by a rancorous hatred of good music could this state of affairs be conceivable. I have bought Waller's

12 "Further Notes on Mauberley," *Accent* xvi (Winter 1956).

poems for a shilling. Yet Lawes' position in English music is proportionally much more important than Waller's position among English poets.

However, as a whole, *Hugh Selwyn Mauberley* is open to the objections that Pound foresaw when, writing to Hardy, he spoke disparagingly of "homage" as "a term of aesthetic *attitude*." Too much of *Hugh Selwyn Mauberley* is *attitudinizing*. The poem is the elaborate culmination of Pound's attempts to be urbane, but urbanity did not come naturally to him; on the contrary, he rather often adopted the wrong stratagems in social situations. Among such stratagems was a range of expedients subsumed by Pound under the name of persona or mask. His protégé Eliot had made brilliant use of the strictly verbal *persona* J. Alfred Prufrock; and his Anglo-Irish mentor, Yeats, was to make brilliant histrionic use of masks called Michael Robartes and Owen Aherne and Crazy Jane. Pound seems to have intended Hugh Selwyn Mauberley to serve him in the same way. But his temperament was quite different from either Eliot's or Yeats's; his treatment of Villon in *The Spirit of Romance* reveals that he responded readily in his reading to a quality of robust self-exposure in poets, precisely what the doctrines of persona and mask were designed to obviate. Accordingly, Hugh Selwyn Mauberley is a mask that continually slips, like Walter Villerant in the *Imaginary Letters* of just the same period. What is the mask for, if, as often as not, the poet throws it off and speaks vulnerably as and from himself? More distractingly still, since we are advised of the mask in the very title, how are we to know in which poems Pound speaks through the mask, in which he doesn't?[13] *Hugh Selwyn Mauberley* remains a very important poem; apart from anything else, it has proved to be the most insidiously and aptly quotable of Pound's poems, and it has very great merit as an Englishing of Gautier.[14] But it looks as if it will figure in Pound's *œuvre* like Gray's "Elegy" in the poetry of Gray—as a relatively early piece which unsympathetic readers can use as a stick with which to beat later work that the poet set more store by.

Homage to Sextus Propertius is a very different matter. In Allen Upward's *The New Word*, the word in question is "idealist," as used by Alfred Nobel when prescribing that his prize for literature should go to "the most distinguished work of an idealist tendency." Quite early in his investigation (in chapter three), Upward decides that "idealist" as thus used is a Babu word. And he explains:

> The English in India . . . have set up schools to train the natives in our ways, and, to begin with, in our speech. There is a very large class of natives called Babus who learn very readily up to a certain point, that is to say, they spell our words correctly, and they have some notion of what the words mean; but English has not replaced their native speech, and hence it fits them like a borrowed garment, and they are betrayed into awkward and laughable mistakes in

[13] An end came to much special pleading on this score when Mrs. Berryman, *loc. cit.*, showed that "Medallion" must be taken as spoken with pride *in propria persona*, though most earlier commentaries (including my own) had supposed it must be uttered in the assumed character of Mauberley.

[14] This was first demonstrated, along with much else of the first importance, by J. J. Espey, *Ezra Pound's Mauberley: A Study in Composition*.

using it, which have given rise to the term Babu English.

I cannot be held responsible for the unworried arrogance with which Upward, in the age of Kipling, speaks of "the natives." The linguistic phenomenon which he describes and names is nonetheless familiar to anyone who has had dealings in ex-colonial territories; presumably there is Babu French and Babu Dutch as well as Babu English. And this is the language that much of *Homage to Sextus Propertius* is written in. How this can be, comes clear if we allow Upward to continue:

> Now that is just the process from which a great part of Europe, and especially England itself, has been suffering for many hundreds of years. Our speech betrays us to be the freedmen of Rome. Our schools are Roman schools set up by missionaries from the Mediterranean in whose minds it was the very aim and end of education to tame the young barbarian of the North into an obedient provincial of the great Roman Raj. . . . Our schools are still called grammar schools, which means Latin-grammar schools, and Latin is the chief thing taught in them. Latin is the official language of our universities, and by an educated man we mean a man who has been taught Latin. The whole theory of our education still is that the young Englishman should make-believe to be an ancient Roman. . . .

Upward, it will be realized, is no Mediterranean-centered man, such as Pound was. Yet he does not, any more than Pound, fly off the handle into the easy and wrong assumptions which since his day have changed Anglophone education beyond recognition, and mostly for the worse: the assumption, for instance, that the

Babu can be "true to himself" only by forgetting his Babu English and reverting to, say, Tamil; or the assumption that, because the paradigms of Latin grammar are foreign to the nature of spoken English, therefore those paradigms have no relevance and no usefulness to us as we try to communicate clearly in our language. Upward does not conclude that, because Nobel's "idealist" is a word foreign to both Swedish and English, it has no meaning in either language. Quite to the contrary. And Pound's practice is quite to the contrary also; that is what is meant by "Make It New." We *do* have access to the Mediterranean wisdoms, and our Babu Latin goes halfway to making the most of that access. It is for asserting that the rest of the way is left to travel, and for traveling that distance on our behalf, that Pound has been, and is, reviled.

Accordingly, it should be clear why Pound's most virulent revilers have been professional classicists, and why *Homage to Sextus Propertius*, along with his translation decades later of the *Women of Trachis* of Sophocles, has been the text of his that has given most offense.[15] For the professor of classics is pre-eminently

[15] The most immediately damaging attack on *Homage to Sextus Propertius* by a classicist was launched by William Gardner Hale, whose censures on part of the poem that had appeared in *Poetry* in March 1919 were partly reproduced in the Chicago *Tribune*. This was damaging because Hale was a friend of Harriet Monroe, who in Chicago, as editor of *Poetry*, had been bullied by Pound into publishing "the new poetry"—an arrangement which now foundered. Pound's version of the *Trachiniae* (in *Hudson Review*, 1954; in book form as *Women of Trachis*, 1956) was discussed by classicists and others in *The Pound Newsletter*, 5 (Berkeley, 1955). Their views are discussed in my *Ezra Pound: Poet as Sculptor*, pp. 233–39.

the Babu, the beneficiary and hence the custodian of a mandarin language acquired in just the way Upward describes. To the professional classicist it seems a matter of life and death to maintain that he has gone, not halfway, but *all* the way. What is involved is social and economic status, precisely as in Anglo-India—hence the way that such critics harp upon "dignity."[16] What Pound renders from Propertius as "Death has its tooth in the lot" had years before been translated by him into acceptable Babu English, thoroughly dignified and thoroughly bland—as he pointed out good-naturedly, when replying to a genial but sharp reviewer.[17] In all seriousness it can be said that when, even leaving aside the professional classicists, we confront Robert Nichols' review of 1920 or, decades later, attacks on *Homage to Sextus Propertius* by Robert Graves and Robert Conquest,[18] what we have to deal with is the entire snarled complex of feelings that we encounter in Frantz Fanon or in the timid and inconclusive suggestions of the young (Algerian) Camus. Every white-skinned English-

---

[16] See Frederic Peachy and Richmond Lattimore in *The Pound Newsletter*, 5; and *The New Age*, November 27, 1919: "Unfortunately, Propertius' dignity and passion have also to be forced into this jaunty mould. . . ."

[17] *The New Age*, Vol. 26 (1919): 82–83. Both this reply and the review to which Pound replies are usefully reproduced in J. P. Sullivan, *Ezra Pound and Sextus Propertius: A Study in Creative Translation* (Austin, 1964), pp. 6–10. The earlier version of some crucial Propertius lines appeared in *Canzoni* (1911) as "Prayer for His Lady's Life." Pound calls it, accurately, "a perfectly literal and, by the same token, perfectly lying and . . . mendacious translation."

[18] Robert Nichols, "Poetry and Mr Pound," *The Observer* (Sunday, January 11, 1920); Robert Graves, "These Be Your Gods," in *The Crowning Privilege* (New York, 1956); Robert Conquest, in *The London Magazine* (April 1963).

speaker, however used he may be to regarding himself as a *colon* (colonist), has also been *colonisé* (colonized). The evidence is in our language, as soon as we set it beside Latin; and just that, I suggest, explains the passion with which we contemplate such tricks with our language as Pound played in *Homage to Sextus Propertius*.

I have said before that the language of *Homage to Sextus Propertius*, or of much of it, is "translatorese."[19] The term from Upward, "Babu English," makes the same point, and makes it better:

> *The twisted rhombs ceased their clamour of accompaniment;*
> *The scorched laurel lay in the fire-dust;*
> *The moon still declined to descend out of heaven,*
> *But the black ominous owl hoot was audible.*

The absurdly misplaced formality of "declined to" and the ludicrously stilted passive "was audible" exemplify the English of the bored schoolboy lazily construing his Latin homework but, equally, the proudly pompous clerk (Pakistani, Cypriot, or whatever) using the language of those who were lately his imperial masters. The point is a crucial one, for *Homage to Sextus Propertius* is often presented as a model of how to translate, whereas much of the time it is a deliberate model of how not to![20] So far from being a model for translators to follow, it deliberately and consistently incorporates

[19] *Ezra Pound: Poet as Sculptor*, p. 87. John Espey has traced in poems in *Lustra* Pound's discovery and gradual mastery of "the technique of the deliberate howler." *Paideuma*, Vol. 1, no. 1 (1972).
[20] J. P. Sullivan's *Ezra Pound and Sextus Propertius*, though valuable, is vitiated by this assumption that Pound's dealings with Propertius are a model of what the translator's

*mis*translation—the "awkward and laughable mistakes"
that the Babu inevitably makes:

> *These are your images, and from you* the sorcerizing
> of shut-in young ladies. . . .
> *No barbarism would* go to the extent of *doing him
> harm*. . . .
> *Who so indecorous as to* shed the pure gore of a
> suitor. . . .
> 'Death why tardily come?! . .
> *Have you* contempted *Juno's Pelasgian temples* . . . ?
> *Zeus' clever rapes, in the old days,*
>   combusted *Semele's, of Io*
>   *strayed*. . . .

In each of these lines I have romanized the words which
seem unmistakably Babu English or "translatorese,"
examples of "how not to do it." It is most often a case of
unsuitably heightened diction; and this accounts for
hilarious passages in an idiom which we have learned
to call, since Pound's day, "camp." But sometimes, as in
the fourth example above, the comical oddity is not in
the vocabulary so much as in word order and syntax,
as in:

> *Sailor, of winds; a plowman, concerning his oxen;*
> *Soldier, the enumeration of wounds; the sheep-feeder,*
> *of ewes;*
> *We, in our narrow bed, turning aside from battles:*
> *Each man where he can, wearing out the day in his*
> *manner.*

---

should be with his original; a doubtless more dangerously
influential statement of the same error is in George Steiner's
Introduction to his *Penguin Book of Modern Translated
Verse* (London, 1966). Pound has indeed renovated the art
of verse translation in our time, but this is not one of the
works by which he did so!

(Here the deliberate incongruity of reproducing in a relatively uninflected language the word order and syntax of a highly inflected one produces a comic effect which, with a mastery that is the peculiar glory of this poem, modulates into profound and plangent feeling. And this is a way of saying that the Babu is a hopeful and suffering human creature, no less than the rest of us.)

Every one of these examples of mistranslation can be detected as such by an attentive and halfway sophisticated reader of the English. There is no need to check back to the Latin text of Propertius. But Pound, for good measure, deliberately planted ludicrous howlers, to amuse those who knew the Latin or chose to consult it. This was a miscalculation, given the pompousness and prickliness of the Babu mentality. ("Propertius Soliloquizes" might have saved Pound some of the storm that broke over his head, but not much.) The Babus were *not* amused, and they remain unreconciled to the present day; we've already seen why they would. Wyndham Lewis in 1920, writing to *The Observer* to protest at Robert Nichols' review, made the essential point: "Mr Pound . . . may conceivably know that Chaucer, Landor, Ben Jonson, and many contemporaries of Rowlandson found other uses for classic texts than that of making literal English versions of them." And Lewis points out that Pound's poem parodies Yeats at one point, and names Wordsworth at another.[21] But he cannot nail what is insupportable about Nichols, because what is insupportable is Nichols' *tone*. Nichols is well informed, and some of his information deserves more considera-

[21] *The Observer* (January 18, 1920).

tion than Poundians have given it—the fact, for instance, that Propertius was Thomas Campion's favorite Latin poet, and that Campion or some other described him as a poet of "melancholy remembrance and vesperal," which is not altogether the impression Pound gives of him. But Nichols' information goes for nothing because it is offered sneeringly, in a tone of vindictive insolence which thinly papers over a wounded sense of personal and professional affront. It is the very tone of Gifford in the *Quarterly* reviewing Keats's *Endymion*. It is the tone of the Babu. And in a sense it proves that the poem has struck home. For all the manifold ironies of *Homage to Sextus Propertius* are directed ultimately at the reader, who is convicted, line by line, of having only pompously imperial, Babu English, into which to render a poem that derides and deflates imperial pretensions. Thus it appears that by wholly transposing "imperialism" into language, into the texture of style, by forgetting his own existence "for the sake of the lines," Pound has effected a far more wounding and penetrating critique of imperialism in general than he could have done by fabricating consciously a schematic correspondence between himself and Propertius, the British Empire and the Roman.

Ideas in *The Cantos*

•

IV

Pound said he had been mulling over a scheme for *The Cantos* from as early as 1904. After a false start in 1919, they appeared in book form, several cantos at a time, from 1925 to 1967. Those who know them by hearsay—and few know them any other way—will think they can declare at least some of the ideas of the poem. That usury is a vicious and desolating force in both public and private life; that it may be defined in such-and-such a way; that it has operated in recorded history after such-and-such a fashion; that international Jewry has played, and continues to play, such-and-such a crucial part in its operations; that Mussolini, unlike Roosevelt, had a grasp of what usury was and had a practicable plan for containing and disinfecting it—such, hearsay reports, are among the ideas which *The Cantos* incorporate, if indeed they are not the ideas which *The Cantos* were written to promote.

And yet these, it may be said, are not ideas at all, but opinions. For "opinions" read "convictions," and the case is not altered. An opinion or a conviction is something we *hold by*. An opinion is to be reckoned with according as it is a *fixed* opinion; a conviction, according as it is *firm*. And we have need of such fixities. The need is not to be denied or deplored. As Allen Upward said, "The nature of Matter is Fixity, and it has no more ultimate nature than this. The ultimate nature of Materialism is the worship of Fixity, under a hundred names, whether Matter or Shape, Exactness or Certainty, or Rest or Death." Pound himself had been much enamored of the sort of fixity called "exactness." And indeed, because we have a need of such fixities, materialism, as Upward understands the term, is no dishonorable banner to fight under—particularly since, as theoretical physics was demonstrating already in 1908, the fixities that scrupulous materialists discover are in any case vibrant, the locking together of opposing forces:

The Cross is the Sign of Matter, and as such it reminds us of the nature of Matter. Not only is it the rude picture of a knot . . . but it shows us how the knot is made. It is by two lines of string meeting cross-wise. Thus it reminds us that two Ways of Strength must meet cross-wise to become entangled. And their entanglement is their arrest. We know they do not rest. The strain of forward motion turns into the strain of pressure. The soldiers do not halt, but they mark time, and mark it faster than they marched. The wrestlers tremble as they lock.[1]

One may feel that in Pound's poem, when Roosevelt grapples with Mussolini, the bout is rigged; that one of the wrestlers is prevented from exerting his full strength; and accordingly that the fixity of the fixed opinion in favor of Mussolini lacks the vibrancy of the hard-earned fixities we esteem in other poems by other hands—for instance, in Johnson's "The Vanity of Human Wishes," or in *The Divine Comedy*.

But "idea"? Idea is sometihng quite different. To Upward's way of thinking, "idea" is not opinion or conviction either. It is not aimed at fixity:

> The Greek lexicon has not done half its work in telling us that *idea* meant appearance. Even in Plato's time it had got further than that. Aquinas, who wrote in Latin and translates it by the Latin *forma*, explains *idea* as being the builder's plan of a not-yet-built house. Now my Dutch word-book renders "idea" (as an English word) by *ontwerp*, which is to say, outthrow—that which the mind throws out, and not what it takes in. And in Holland a builder's plan is called an *ontwerp*. When the mind of a great Roman theologian jumps with the common mind of a Dutch folk, we ought to be able to take the result with some security. And it is the opposite pole of the meaning given us by the lexicon. The idea is not the appearance of a thing already there, but rather the imagination of a thing not yet there. It is not the look of a thing, it is a looking forward to a thing.[2]

[1] Allen Upward, *The New Word* (London, 1908), Fourteenth Head.
[2] *Ibid.*, Third Head.

There is no doubt in my mind that this was the passage Pound had in mind, more or less consciously and exactly, when he wrote in *Guide to Kulchur*:

> "I made it out of a mouthful of air," wrote Bill Yeats in his heyday. The *forma*, the immortal *concetto*, the concept, the dynamic form which is like the rose pattern driven into the dead iron-filings by the magnet, not by material contact with the magnet itself, but separate from the magnet. Cut off by the layer of glass, the dust and filings rise and spring into order. Thus the *forma*, the concept rises from death. . . .[3]

And there is an unmistakably equivalent passage in *The Pisan Cantos* (Canto 74):

> Hast 'ou seen the rose in the steel dust
> (or swansdown ever?)
> so light is the urging, so ordered the dark petals of
> iron
> we who have passed over Lethe.

Thus it seems that we might, and probably should, hark back to the initial formulation by Upward, and declare that when we look for ideas in *The Cantos*, we should look for the *forma* and the *ontwerp*, for "ideas" in the sense we have when we say, "I have an idea for a poem" or, more simply still, "I've a great idea—why don't we all go to the beach on Tuesday?" These are "ideas" as we meet them, interestingly enough, in the pages of Longinus; not ideas *of* (for example, to take Pound's word for it for the moment, an idea of what American history has been since 1913, when with the founding

---

[3] *Guide to Kulchur*, in the New Directions reprint (1952), p. 152.

of the Federal Reserve Bank the United States flouted the constitutional duty to issue money) but ideas *for* (for example, an idea for an America that should have risen in revolt against this and antecedent usurious trickeries).

If this seems like restricting "idea" in *The Cantos* to mean merely free-floating and utopian *aspiration*, another look at the pages of Upward will disabuse us. For Upward has too much respect for the honest materialist —in particular, for the physicist of his day—to forget, when he turns to look at the *im*materialist (or as he must call him, following Alfred Nobel, the *idealist*), how the materialist conceives of matter as knotted and equally opposed strengths, as in the wrestlers who tremble as they lock.[4] This *is* the nature of matter; and in Upward's view the idealist—we may as well call him the poet—must acknowledge this as freely as the physicist does. But the poet asks: What follows? And to answer that, Upward abandons the model of the two locked wrestlers, and deploys instead a range of models —the vortex, the waterspout, the legendary tree Yggdrasil, at the furthest reach and most abstrusely the crystal —all of which are to figure in *The Cantos*, for the most part thirty or forty years after Pound first read *The New Word*. The model that Upward explains most fully is the special sort of vortex, or double vortex, that is called a waterspout:

[4] Pound, it should be said, shared Upward's respect for experimental science, especially for biologists. Agassiz, Von Humboldt, Fabre, Mme. Curie, and Frobenius were among his "heroes of modern science." And it was Gourmont's most "scientific" book, *Physique de L'amour* (Paris, 1904) that Pound chose to translate as *The Natural Philosophy of Love* (New York, 1922).

The story of the waterspout, as it is told in books, shows it to be a brief-lived tree. A cloud is whirling downwards, and thrusting out its whirlpoint towards the sea, like a sucking mouth. The sea below whirls upwards, thrusting out its whirlpoint towards the cloud. The two ends meet, and the water swept up in the sea-whirl passes on into the cloud-whirl, and swirls up through it, as it were gain-saying it. . . .

In the ideal waterspout, not only does the water swirl upwards through the cloud-whirl, but the cloud swirls downwards through the sea-whirl. . . .

The ideal waterspout is not yet complete. The upper half must unfold like a fan, only it unfolds all around like a flower-cup; and it does not leave the cup empty, so that this flower is like a chrysanthemum. At the same time the lower half has unfolded in the same way, till there are two chrysanthemums back to back. . . .

It is strength turning inside out. Such is the true beat of strength, the first beat, the one from which all others part, the beat which we feel in all things that come within our measure, in ourselves, and in our starry world. . . .

Upward did not live to see this inspired guess at "the first beat" astonishingly confirmed experimentally, when the biophysicists Crick and Watson broke the genetic code to reveal "the double helix" (that is to say, double vortex). And Upward, it should be plain, did not laxly abandon the figure of the locked wrestlers as soon as it got him into difficulties. The two wrestlers survive into this more elaborate model, under the names of Whirl and Swirl. Given that neither wrestler can throw the other, what happens to the energy which each of them is exerting? It must go somewhere. And the

answer is that Whirl and Swirl, as they are locked ever-
more tensely, tighten into a cone, at the apex of which
"strength turns inside out," Swirl becomes Whirl and
Whirl becomes Swirl, and an inverted cone grows out of
the first one. Readers of Yeats's *A Vision* will recognize
a very similar model in his diagram of interlocking and
overlapping gyres; if not in Upward himself, then in
G. R. S. Mead or else in the Chaldean thaumaturges
whom Mead and Upward agreed in studying, Yeats
must have found his source.[5] And in Yeats and Pound
alike the "idea *for*" is governed just as imperiously by
this paradigm of "turning inside out" as is "idea *of*" by
the ascertainable facts of that which the idea (in this
other sense) is allegedly copying.

In *The Pound Era*[6] Hugh Kenner has made striking
use of the knot, in terms of Buckminster Fuller's concepts of "self-interfering patterns" and "patterned in-
tegrity," to characterize the forms that Pound and
Wyndham Lewis, from 1913 onward, were seeking to
create. But Upward, it will be recognized, forestalled
this perception; he acknowledged "self-interfering pat-
tern" (the term is not Upward's, but the perception is)
as indeed of the nature of a knot, in the sense of that
"knotting" or "matting" from which he derived the very
word "matter," and acknowledged the truth of this
model for "form" in nature; yet at the same time he
protested that to see "form" thus was to make an ar-
bitrarily arrested cross section of what was in fact and
in experience a continuous process—a process by which
locked energies narrow into a cone, reverse themselves

[5] I am not aware that these possibilities have been investigated.
[6] Hugh Kenner, *The Pound Era*, pp. 145–46.

at its apex, and thereafter flower upside-down and inside-out.

The reversal, more precisely the introversion, at the point where a new cone or gyre springs out of the tense apex of the first (the point where, in Upward's vocabulary, Swirl and Whirl change places) is managed in the language of *The Cantos* in many different ways. Often it is signaled by a change of tense and of grammatical mood in verbs. This is particularly common in the sequel to the Pisan sequence, those *Rock-Drill* cantos where it may be thought that the writing of *The Cantos* is at its most daring, assured, and splendid. Canto 91, for instance, begins with two lines of music in archaic notation set to words in Provençal. Then it continues:

> *that the body of light come forth*
> > *from the body of fire*
> *And that your eyes come to the surface*
> > *from the deep wherein they were sunken,*
> *Reina—for 300 years*
> > *and now sunken*
> *That your eyes come forth from their caves*
> > *& light then*
> > > *as the holly-leaf*
> > > *qui laborat, orat*
> *Thus Undine came to the rock,*
> > > *by Circeo*
> *and the stone eyes again looking seaward*

The first several lines very plainly give us idea as *ontwerp*, as "out-throw," looking forward; the grammatical mood of "come forth," "come to the surface," "come forth" ("from their caves") is, accordingly, optative—they represent what it is hoped will happen, what is willed to happen. And the introduction of such sentiments with "that" (the antecedent "I pray" or "I will" being suppressed) is so common in the late Cantos as to be almost a mannerism. The change of tense and mood into the past indicative of "Thus Undine *came*" represents, I take it, the reversal of the spiral, the turning inside-out. It surely does *not* mean that Undine came to the rock in some time antecedent to the time at which the prayer for her coming is uttered; on the contrary, it seems to mean that the prayer has, at least in imagination, been answered. At the very least, one may say that in a context where prosaic conventions—for instance, of tense sequence—have been so consistently flouted, one cannot expect a past indicative to mean what it means in prose discourse.

I am far from being unaware of the riskiness—not for the poet only, but for his culture—of playing thus fast and loose with the conventions that govern prosaic or spoken discourse. And every one must detect the irony in the fact that the poet who came around to writing like this started from a conviction that poetry had to incorporate (and surpass) prosaic exactness. Just here, in fact, is a parting of the ways: either we suppose that our grasp on cultural order, as reflected in our language, is too insecure for such departures as this to be tolerated, let alone emulated; or else, we do not. For my part, a decision either way—given that the person deciding has recognized just what is at issue—is equally honorable.

With all of this, it must not be supposed that Pound is slavishly dependent on Upward as his source and his authority. On the contrary, he has a fundamental quarrel with him; for Pound defined himself as "Mediterranean man"—a description that never appears in Upward's pages without an unmistakable note of hostility. Upward, as we know him from his writing (and I am aware of no document that allows us to know him otherwise, so firmly has he been consigned to oblivion), is on the one hand thoroughly a distinguished child of his generation, master of a trenchant clarity that takes no care not to be overbearing, any more than Chesterton's clarity does, or George Bernard Shaw's; but on the other hand, Upward is—quite consciously, one must suppose—a Carlylean figure, ranging himself (at times like a proto-Nazi) on the side of Nordic or Baltic or Scandinavian folk-wisdom against Greco-Roman pretensions. And with this Pound could have no sympathy. Thus, whereas Upward is impatient with Greco-Roman mythology ("It is bad language . . . because it is out of date, and we repeat it without understanding it, like the Latin-school boys, and their Oxford schoolmasters"), Pound consistently, and increasingly as the years go on, applies himself to interpreting classical myth. Yet Upward, twenty years after he had died by his own despairing hand in 1926, remained a redoubtable opponent for Pound to contend with. In 1946, in the detention camp at Pisa, Pound remembered a page of *The New Word* which Upward had devoted to showing how he could have beaten the classicists at their own game, if he had thought it worthwhile:

How hard the old cloistered scholarship . . . has toiled to understand the word *glaukopis*, given to the goddess Athene. Did it mean blue-eyed, or gray-eyed, or —by the aid of Sanskrit—merely glare-eyed? And all the time they had not only the word *glaux* staring them in the face, as the Athenian name for owl, and the name of ox-eyed Hera to guide them, but they had the owl itself cut at the foot of every statue of Athene, and stamped on every coin of Athens, to tell them that she was the owl-eyed goddess, the lightning that blinks like an owl. For what is characteristic of the owl's eyes is not that they glare, but that they suddenly leave off glaring, like lighthouses whose light is shut off. We may see the shutter of the lightning in that mask that overhangs Athene's brow, and hear its click in the word *glaukos*. And the leafage of the olive, whose writhen trunk bears, as it were, the lightning's brand, does not glare, but glitters, the pale underface of the leaves alternating with the dark upperface, and so the olive in Athene's tree, and is called *glaukos*. Why need we carry owls to Oxford."[7]

This is the passage that was in the poet's mind in the cage at Pisa when, some thirty or forty lines after evoking Upward by name, Pound wrote in Canto 74:

> *Le Paradis n'est pas artificiel*
>   *but spezzato apparently*
> *it exists only in fragments unexpected excellent sausage*
>   *the smell of mint, for example,*
>   *Ladro the night cat;*
> *at Nemi waited on the slope above the lane sunken in the pocket of hills*
> *awaiting decision from the old lunch cabin built out over the shingle,*

[7] Pound drew attention to this page of Upward in a letter (*Selected Letters*, D. D. Paige, ed., p. 357), and an echo of it ("the olives . . . the leaves green and then not green . . . the click of light in their branches") is to be heard as early as Canto 20 (c. 1925). It was quoted in full in Pound's "Allen Upward Serious," *The New Age* (April 23, 1914).

Zarathustra, now desuete
to Jupiter and to Hermes where now is the castellaro
  no vestige save in the air
in stone is no imprint and the grey walls of no era
   under the olives
   saeculorum Athenae
    γλαύξ, γλανκῶπις,
    olivi
that which gleams and then does not gleam
   as the leaf turns in the air

This passage, where "glaux" and "glaukopis" are
given in the Greek, begins with a statement of what we
commonly understand by an "idea," that is to say, an
opinion or conviction asserted in the form of a proposition: "Le Paradis n'est pas artificiel" (Paradise is not
artificial). The assertion carries weight because it is
backed by painful experience; the lines immediately
preceding have made wretched scatological puns on the
dysentery the prisoner was suffering from. But even so,
the assertion is not a simple expression of opinion, however hard-earned; that is why it is in French—it is a
rejoinder to Baudelaire, who gave the title *Les Paradis
Artificiels* to a book about drug-taking. In the same way
"spezzato" (splintered) is in Italian so as to allude to
another expert on Paradise, Dante; for later in this
Canto we are to read:

 By no means an orderly Dantescan rising
 but as the winds veer . . .

Pound finds that his experience of the paradisal is at
odds with Baudelaire's testimony on one hand, Dante's
on the other. But the propositional statement of this is
not to be trusted in any case. It is only the first turn of

a spiral which mounts and tightens through allusions to the similarly splintered and intermittent utterances which we call "oracular" (Lake Nemi is one place where oracles were awaited) and to Athene (goddess of wisdom—thus it is no fool's paradise we are concerned with), and the topmost tightest turn or whirl is on the intermittent glitter of olive leaves, their significance precisely that which Upward had explained.

What is crucial is that we should understand by "idea" in *The Cantos* the whole of this process of circling round and throwing out. (An idea, we might say, is *thrown out*, whereas an opinion is *held by* or *held on to*.) The whole of this process, and indeed a little more; for the turning inside-out, the switch into the inverted spiral, comes only in the next lines after those quoted, when the air that the leaf turns in becomes the positive force of *winds*:

> *Boreas Apeliota libeccio*
> 'C'è il babao,' said the young mother
>   and the bathers like small birds under hawk's
>   eye
>   shrank back under the cliff's edge at il Poz-
>   zetto . . .

("Libeccio" is the south wind; and "There it is, the bugbear" is what the young mother says as the wind rises and drives the bathers to find shelter. Her unselfconscious personification of the wind vindicates the anthropomorphizing and mythological habits of the Mediterranean mind, just what Upward was impatient with.)

What is fatal, though it is very common, is to regard the idea as having been stated in the initial proposition;

and the verses which follow—Lake Nemi, Athene, the olives—as supplying no more than embroidery upon the idea, at best illustrations or elaborations of it. Read in that way, the *Cantos* are merely boring. They were found so by the late Yvor Winters, who, conceiving of an idea as that which could be stated in the form of a proposition, recorded his experience of reading *The Cantos* by saying, "We have no way of knowing whether we have had any ideas or not."[8] Winters meant to be dismissive and disparaging; but in fact, if we take account of what he understood "idea" to be, Winters' remark is one of the few valuably exact formulations that we have, of what reading *The Cantos* amounts to, and feels like.

As we start to read *The Cantos*, we float out upon a sea where we must be on the lookout for waterspouts. These, when they occur, are ideas, the only sort that this poem is going to give us. And meanwhile we can forget about such much-debated nonquestions as whether this poem has a structure, and if so, what it is: or again, why the poem isn't finished, and whether it ever could have been. Does a sea have a *structure*? Does a sea *finish* anywhere? The Mediterranean boils into and out of the Atlantic, past the Rock of Gibraltar.

As for the final reach of Upward's interpretation—beyond olive leaves in the wind, to *lightning*—we come to it in the *Rock-Drill* Canto 92:

Le Paradis n'est pas artificiel
> *but is jagged,*

For a flash,

8 Yvor Winters, *The Function of Criticism* (Denver, 1957), p. 47.

for an hour.
Then agony,
then an hour,
then agony,
Hilary stumbles, but the Divine Mind is abundant
unceasing
improvisatore
Omniformis
unstill . . .

And Canto 95 begins:

LOVE, gone as lightning,
enduring 5000 years.

Rhythms in *The Cantos*

V

Every student of *The Cantos* knows how insidiously their method of "juxtaposition without copula"[1] persuades the commentator also into presenting his findings in the form of mere tabulation, or of "specimens" pinned side by side in a display case. But I think I shall not be wasting the reader's time if I present him with seven specimens:

[1] This "method," if it deserves that name, is more often described as "ideogrammic" or "ideographic." Its theoretical justification is in Ernest Fenollosa's essay, "The Chinese Written Character as a Medium for Poetry." This important essay, in Pound's redaction, first appeared in *The Little Review* in 1919, and was reprinted in *Instigations*, 1920. I have discussed it in my *Articulate Energy: An Inquiry into the Syntax of English Poetry* (New York, 1955), chap. 4.

(1) from Ben Jonson's *A Celebration of Charis:
in Ten Lyric Pieces* (1624), the fourth of those
pieces, "Her Triumph":

See the chariot at hand here of Love
   Wherein my Lady rideth!
Each that draws is a swan or a dove,
   And well the car Love guideth.
As she goes all hearts do duty
   Unto her beauty;
And enamoured do wish, so they might
   But enjoy such a sight,
That they still were to run by her side
Thorough swords, thorough seas,
   whither she would ride.

Do but look on her eyes, they do light
   All that Love's world compriseth!
Do but look on her hair, it is bright
   As Love's star when it riseth!
Do but mark, her forehead's smoother
   Than words that soothe her;
And from her arched brows such a grace
   Sheds itself through the face,
As alone there triumphs to the life
All the gain, all the good, of the elements' strife.

Have you seen but a bright lily grow
   Before rude hands have touched it?
Ha' you marked but the fall o' the snow
   Before the soil hath smutched it?
Ha' you felt the wool of beaver
   Or swan's down ever?
Or have smelt o' the bud o' the briar?
   Or the nard in the fire?
Or have tasted the bag of the bee?
O so white! O so soft! O so sweet is she!

(2) from Canto XLVII (1937):

> *And the small stars now fall from the olive branch,*
> *Forked shadow falls dark on the terrace*
> *More black than the floating martin*
> > *that has no care for your presence,*
> *His wing-print is black on the roof tiles*
> *And the print is gone with his cry.*
> *So light is thy weight on Tellus*
> *Thy notch no deeper indented*
> *Thy weight less than the shadow*
> *Yet hast thou gnawed through the mountain,*
> > *Scilla's white teeth less sharp.*
> *Hast thou found a nest softer than cunnus*
> *Or hast thou found better rest*
> *Hast'ou a deeper planting, doth thy death year*
> *Bring swifter shoot?*
> *Hast thou entered more deeply the mountain?*
>
> *The light has entered the cave. Io! Io!*
> *The light has gone down into the cave,*
> *Splendour on splendour!*
> *By prong have I entered these hills:*
> *That the grass grow from my body,*
> *That I hear the roots speaking together,*
> *The air is new on my leaf,*
> *The forked boughs shake with the wind. . . .*

(3) Canto LXXIV (a Pisan Canto, 1948):

> *the useful operations of commerce*
> > *stone after stone of beauty cast down*
> *and authenticities disputed by parasites*
> > > *(made in Ragusa) and: what art do you*
> > > *handle?*
> *'The best' And the moderns? 'Oh, nothing modern*
> *we couldn't sell anything modern.'*

But Herr Bacher's father made madonnas still in the
    tradition[2]
carved wood as you might have found in any cathedral
          and another Bacher still cut intaglios
                  such as Salustio's in the time of
                Ixotta,
where the masks come from, in the Tirol,
    in the winter season
        searching every house to drive out the demons.
Serenely in the crystal jet
        as the bright ball that the fountain tosses
(Verlaine) as diamond clearness
        How soft the wind under Taishan
            where the sea is remembered
    out of hell, the pit
    out of the dust and glare evil
    Zephyrus / Apeliota
This liquid is certainly a
        property of the mind
nec accidens est   but an element
                in the mind's make-up
est agens and functions   dust to the fountain pan
                      otherwise
        Hast 'ou seen the rose in the steel dust
              (or swansdown ever?)
so light is the urging, so ordered the dark petals of
                      iron
we who have passed over Lethe.

(4) Canto LXXX (another Pisan Canto, 1948):

hast'ou swum in a sea of air strip
    through an aeon of nothingness,
when the raft broke and the waters went over me,

[2] The details about Herr Bacher's father, like others about
folk-customs in the Austrian Tirol, come from the Tirolean
village where Pound's natural daughter, Mary, was reared

Immaculata, Introibo
  for those who drink of the bitterness
Perpetua, Agatha, Anastasia
          saeculorum

repos donnez à cils
        senza termine funge   Immaculata Regina[3]
        Les larmes que j'ai créées m'inondent
Tard, très tard je t'ai connue, la Tristesse,
I have been hard as youth sixty years. . . .

(5) Canto LXXXI (another Pisan Canto, 1948):

  a leaf in the current
            at my grates no Althea

---

by foster parents. See Mary de Rachewiltz, *Discretions* (Boston, 1971).

[3] The word *funge*, which is to be found in Cantos 74 and 85 as well as here, is not in the *della' Crusca* dictionary or in other Italian dictionaries; nor is it found in Dante. Hugh Kenner ran it to earth in Pound's Italian translation of Confucius, *Ciung Iung, L'Asse Che Non Vacilla* (1945): "La purezza funge (nel tempo e nello spazio) senza termine. Senza termine funge, luce tensile"; *Paideuma*, Vol. 1, no. 1 (1972). In Pound's English translation of the same year, *The Unwobbling Pivot*, this becomes: "The *unmixed* functions (in time and in space) without bourne. This unmixed is the tensile light, the Immaculata. There is no end to its action." Mary de Rachewiltz suggests that the coined word *funge* has to do with a program espoused by some Italian Fascists, for putting back into Italian some Latin roots which had dropped out. Thus *funge* means "functions." Pound not only draws on several languages and makes mistakes in them (sometimes deliberately, often not) but also neologizes in them!

In these lines as in *The Pisan Cantos* generally, the framing of the poet's most betrayingly personal confessions in French apparently testifies to a positively Jamesian hauteur and fastidiousness, in Pound's domestic circle, about the naked expression of painful and exacting feeling. On this, some pages of Mary de Rachewiltz's *Discretions* are revealing.

LIBRETTO Yet
Ere the season died a-cold
Borne upon a zephyr's shoulder
I rose through the aureate sky

      Lawes and Jenkyns
        guard thy rest
      Dolmetsch ever be thy
        guest,

Has he tempered the viol's wood
To enforce   both the grave   and the
   acute?
Has he curved us the bowl of the lute?

      Lawes and Jenkyns
        guard thy rest
      Dolmetsch ever be
        thy guest

Hast 'ou fashioned so airy a mood
   To draw up leaf from the root?
Hast 'ou found   a cloud   so light
   As seemed neither mist nor shade?

      Then resolve me,
        tell me aright
      If Waller sang or
        Dowland played,

     Your eyen two wol sleye me
       sodenly
     I may the beauté of hem nat
       susteyne

And for 180 years almost nothing.

(6) Canto 110 (1970):

Thy quiet house
The crozier's curve runs in the wall,

The harl, feather-white, as a dolphin on sea-brink

I am all for Verkehr without tyranny
>   *—wake exultant*
>   *in caracole*
Hast 'ou seen boat's wake on sea-wall
>   *how crests it?*

What panache?
>   *paw-flap, wave-tap,*
>   *that is gaiety,*

Toba Sojo,
>   *toward limpidity,*
>   *that is exultance,*
>   *here the crest runs on wall*
che paion' si al vent'

(7) Basil Bunting, *Briggflatts* (1966):

Flying fish follow the boat,
delicate wings blue, grace
on flick of a tissue tail,
the water's surface between
appetite and attainment.
Flexible, unrepetitive line
to sing, not paint; sing, sing,
laying the tune on the air,
nimble and easy as a lizard,
still and sudden as a gecko,
to humiliate love, remember
nothing.

It tastes good, garlic and salt in it,
with the half-sweet white wine of Orvieto
on scanty grass under great trees
where the ramparts cuddle Lucca.

It sounds right, spoken on the ridge
between marine olives and hillside

blue figs, under the breeze fresh
with pollen of Apennine sage.

It feels soft, weed thick in the cave
and the smooth wet riddance of Antonietta's
bathing suit, mouth ajar for
submarine Amalfitan kisses.

It looks well on the page, but never
well enough. Something is lost
when wind, sun, sea upbraid
justly an unconvinced deserter.

Exegesis will be resisted; I could explicate each of these passages, but our present concern is with rhythm. It is obvious that the catching up and echoing—over intervals of sometimes many hundred verse lines, sometimes only a few score—of a *motif* like Jonson's "Have you seen. . . ?" or "Have you marked. . . ?" constitutes one of the large-scale rhythms that ride through the *Cantos* in our experience of them when we read many at a time, and fast. And this is the sort of reading we ought to give them—not just to begin with, either. This, indeed, is what irritates so many readers and fascinates an elect few—that the *Cantos*, erudite though they are, consistently frustrate the sort of reading that is synonymous with "study," reading such as goes on in the seminar room or the discussion group. It is hopeless to go at them cannily, not moving on to line three until one is sure of line two. They must be taken in big gulps or not at all. Does this means reading without comprehension? Yes, if by comprehension we mean a set of propositions that can be laid end to end. We are in the position of not knowing "whether we have had any ideas or not." Just so. Which is not to deny that some teasing out of quite short excerpts, even some hunting up of sources and allusions, is profitable at some stage. For the *Cantos* are a poem to be lived with, over years. Yet after many years, each new reading—if it is a reading of many pages at a time, as it should be—is a new bewilderment. So it should be, for so it was meant to be. After all, some kinds of bewilderment are fruitful. To one such kind we give the name "awe"—not awe at the poet's accomplishment, his energy, or his erudition but awe at the energies, some human and some nonhuman, which interact, climb, spiral, reverse themselves, and disperse, in the forming and re-forming spectacles which the poet's art presents to us or reminds us of.

This description does not apply to the last specimen, the verses by Bunting (though there are other passages of *Briggflatts* to which it might apply). And it may be merely fanciful to hear in Bunting's "It tastes good," "It sounds right," "It feels soft," "It looks well," a reminiscence of Jonson's "Have you felt. . .?" "Have you smelt. . . ?" But though the particular instance may be ill-chosen, *Briggflatts* is one of a few poems which present themselves under the auspices not just of Pound but specifically of the *Cantos* (the others are all American, and Charles Olson's *Maximus Poems* is the obvious candidate). And when Bunting writes of the "flexible, unrepetitive line/ to sing, not paint; sing, sing/ laying the tune on the air," he is, as we may guess from his other writings, honoring the *cantabile* art practiced by Lawes and Jenkyns, by Waller and Dowland and Lovelace, in the seventeenth century, as by Arnold Dolmetsch and Pound (and Raymonde Collignon) in the twentieth—just the art that is celebrated in our fifth excerpt, from Canto 81, where the memory of Jonson's

cadence not only informs but is the substance of the
verses of lute music which incorporate it.

And· what has this to do with rhythm? Why, this:
that just such discontinuous transmission of shapings
and perceptions over gaps of many centuries—from
Provence to Italy to Chaucer ("Your eyen two wol sleye
me sodenly . . ."), to Campion and Jonson, Lovelace and
Waller, to Pound and Bunting—are the rhythms per-
ceptible in recorded history, or in as much of history as
matters. Pound defined *The Cantos* as "epic," and defined "epic" as "a poem containing history." We have
not much pondered the possible meanings of "containing." One way by which a poem might be thought to
"contain" history is by mirroring in its own large-scale
rhythms the rhythms of discovery, wastage, neglect,
and rediscovery that the historical records give us notice
of. The discoveries and rediscoveries are not of "art
forms," except insofar as we mean by those forms (as,
of course, we always should but seldom do) ways of
feeling, of responsiveness. Moreover, when Pound in
Mauberley spoke of "conservation of the 'better tradition,'" he put the last two words between quotation
marks, thereby baffling many commentators who assumed that when they· detected two traditions at work
in a given period, they were in duty bound to decide
which is "the better"; to decide, for instance, that in the
English seventeenth century the "better tradition" is
illustrated by Donne and Herbert and Marvell, not by
Campion or Dowland, Lovelace or Waller. (Jonson, as
a completely accomplished poet, has an honorable place
in both traditions, so he is an embarrassment who is
best left out of account!) "Tradition" as rhythm working through history—which is how Pound understands

it—will not lend itself to such puerilities. *All* the traditions are precious; they do not compete; and none of them is ever lost beyond recovery, though other rhythms detectable in politico-economic history may work out so that in certain ages some valuable traditions of responsiveness can be recovered only by isolated individuals going painfully against the grain of their times.

But Bunting's "flexible, unrepetitive line" sends us to look at rhythm on a much smaller scale, in each verse line or a brief sequence of such lines; to the run and fall of such lines as spoken, felt in the articulating mouth and in the attentive ear. And here the differences must be glaring between Jonson's verse, which is "metrical," and Pound's or Bunting's, which is "free." Well, *are* they? To be sure, Jonson's three strophes as printed are intricately symmetrical, but is "symmetrical" the same as "repetitive"? More to the point, if Jonson's poem is carefully and intelligently spoken, do we *hear* any one line repeating any other? There *is* repetition, in fact, and the symmetry between the three strophes is Jonson's, not his printer's; but the repetition is "with variations," variations so audacious and inventive that a twentieth-century ear is baffled by them, and few modern readers of Jonson can, when challenged, scan his poem. (For what it is worth, and for whoever cares any longer, the odd lines of Jonson's strophe I take to be anapaestic trimeter; of the even lines, lines two and four are iambic trimeter, line six is iambic dimeter, line eight is anapaestic dimeter, and line ten is anapaestic tetrameter—but all of them with every variation and inversion possible. Pound's sustained allusion in Canto 81 reproduces with great accomplishment the alternation of trisyllabic with disyllabic—in Pound's handling,

mostly trochaic—measures.) Undoubtedly, the order
that persists under the freedoms, in Jonson's writing,
gives an additional exquisite pleasure to the ear that
discerns it, and it has vast implications, ultimately
metaphysical ones. But since so few modern ears can
discern it, it is dishonest to make a great issue out of
it, as when the freedoms that Pound and Bunting take
are denounced as "license" or applauded as "liberation."

To know Pound's considered opinions on prosody, the
obvious place to go is to his "Treatise on Metre," an
appendix to his *ABC of Reading* (1934). But a better
place to start is his review of Eliot's *Prufrock and Other
Observations*, where we come upon the celebrated pro-
nouncement:

> Unless a man can put some thematic invention into
> *vers libre*, he would perhaps do well to stick to "regu-
> lar" metres, which have certain chances of being
> musical from their form, and certain other chances
> of being musical through his failure in fitting the
> form. In *vers libre* his musical chances are but in
> sensitivity and invention.[4]

It is wonderfully good horse sense, and should be required reading for every up-and-coming *avant-gardiste*
poet who scorns to write in regular meters but does not
understand that he has thereby promised some "thematic invention," and has claimed to have, not just
"sensitivity" (that, we are all sure of having) but
"invention" also. Yet this is one of the surprisingly few
places where Pound's arrogance is not just in appearance and tone but in substance also. For he did not take
his own advice—not even in *Mauberley*, where the ap-

[4] *Poetry* (1917), reprinted in *Instigations* (1920).

pearance of metrical quatrains is largely illusory. Pound
knew that he *was* capable of "thematic invention," and
of "sensitivity" (not at all to the pathos of his own pre-
dicaments but to the sound-value of syllables in suc-
cession). This advice is proffered accordingly not to
himself, and if not to the world at large then presumably to Eliot, his esteemed *confrère*, who has already in
the review been ticked off for making no distinction between *vers libre* and *vers libéré* (since he had declared
that "good *vers libre* was little more than a skillful eva-
sion of the better-known English meters") and for
omitting "all consideration of metres depending on
quantity, alliteration, etc.; . . . as if metres were measured by accent." This is Pound at his most arrogant;
and the arrogance is abundantly justified. The sequel
was to show that indeed Eliot had no ear for verse that
was truly "free" but only for verse that departed—
boldly sometimes, timidly sometimes—from a standard
meter like the Jacobean pentameter. To the end of his
career, *vers libéré* was to be the best that Eliot could
manage—as witness his *Four Quartets*, which have
many virtues, but the wearisome swack or thump of
their mostly accentual meters is not among them.

The same distinction between accentual and quanti-
tative components of meter (between *components of*
meter, not between meters) is insisted on in the "Treatise on Metre": "Great obfuscation spread from the
failure to dissociate heavy accent and duration." And
Pound goes on:

So called dactylic hexameter does NOT start from
ONE type of verse.

There are, mathematically, sixty-four basic general
forms of it; of which twenty or thirty were probably

found to be of most general use, and several of which
would probably have been stunts or rarities.

But this takes no count either of shifting caesura
(pause at some point in the line), nor does it count
any of the various shadings.

It ought to be clear that the variety starting FROM
a colony of sixty-four different general rhythm shapes,
or archetypes, will be vastly more compendious, will
naturally accommodate a vastly greater amount of
real speech, than will a set of variants starting from
a single type of line, whether measured by duration
or by the alternating heaviness of syllables,

        specifically:

        ti tum ti tum ti tum ti tum ti tum

from which every departure is treated as an exception.

The authority for Pound's observations on the dactylic
hexameter is apparently—he supplies the reference
himself—the article on Greek metric in the Laurencie
et Lavignac *Encyclopédie de la musique et Dictionnaire
du Conservatoire*. But before the English reader ex-
claims, in the very accents of Mr. Podsnap, "Not English!" he should remember the dactylic hexameter of
Hardy's "In Tenebris III," and the other Greek meters
that Hardy imitated; and he might ask himself whether
in Hardy's poetry as a whole the pentameter line or the
iambic foot is any more common than in Pound's as a
whole. Hardy might have agreed with Pound that "when
the Greek dramatists developed or proceeded from anterior Greek prosody, they arrived at chorus forms
which are to all extents [*sic*] 'free,' though a superstruc-
ture of nomenclature has been gummed on to them by
analysers whom neither Aeschylus nor Euripides would
ever have been bothered to read." As we have seen,

when Pound sent Hardy his *Homage to Sextus Propertius*, it wasn't Pound's versification that the older poet
was bothered by. Yet Hardy might have thought that
Pound's assertion about the Greek dramatists, though
it was probably true, was decidedly rash, since it
seemed to allow to the untrained and insensitive ear
as much authority as to the trained one; and that the
pedantic nomenclature could have some use, as a way
for the dull ear to train itself into keenness.

In any case, these observations too had been anticipated by Pound in his review of Eliot in 1917, when he
wrote:

Alexandrine and other grammarians have made
cubby-holes for various groupings of syllables; they
have put names upon them, and have given various
labels to "metres" consisting of combinations of these
different groups. Thus it would be hard to escape
contact with some group or other; only an encyclo-
pedist could ever be half sure he had done so. The
known categories would allow a fair liberty to the
most conscientious traditionalist. The most fanatical
vers-librist will escape them with difficulty. However,
I do not think there is any crying need for verse with
absolutely no rhythmical basis.

On the other hand I do not believe that Chopin
wrote to a metronome. There is undoubtedly a sense
of music that takes count of the "shape" of the rhythm
in a melody rather than of bar divisions, which came
rather late in the history of written music and were
certainly not the first or most important things that
musicians attempted to record. The creation of such
shapes is part of thematic invention. Some musicians
have the faculty of invention, rhythmic, melodic.
Likewise some poets.

However, there is a statement anterior to the review of 1917, not to speak of *ABC of Reading*, which may be more important than either. Historically, it certainly is, since it is plainly the source of Charles Olson's *Projective Verse*, an essay which has had incomparable importance for serious verse writers in America through the past quarter-century. This statement consists of the last paragraphs of Pound's essay on Dante from *The Spirit of Romance*, paragraphs which he pointedly reprinted in 1937 in the last pages of his *Polite Essays*:

> This government of speed is a very different thing from the surge and sway of the epic music where the smoother rhythm is so merged with the sound quality as to be inextricable. The two things compare almost as the rhythm of a drum compares to the rhythm (not the sound) of the violin or organ. Thus, the "surge and sway" are wonderful in Swinburne's first chorus in the *Atalanta*; while the other quality of word motion is most easily distinguished in, though by no means confined to, such poems as Burns's "Birks o' Aberfeldy," where the actual sound-quality of the words contributes little or nothing to an effect dependent on the arrangement of quantities (i.e. the durations of syllables) and accent. It is not, as might first seem, a question of vowel music as opposed to consonant music.

And this takes us back to where we started from. For, after all, how discuss verse for singing in any of the dialects of English, without mentioning Burns? Though the *Cantos* are "epic," rather few of them display "the surge and sway of the epic music." (Canto 1 displays it, as does our excerpt from Canto 47; and so we respond to these without much trouble.) For the most part the rhythms of the *Cantos*—as in all my other excerpts, though not equally in all—are the sung rhythms of Burns, not the intoned or chanted rhythms of Swinburne.

And so the verse lines of the *Cantos* have to be read *fast* for their meanings, but *slow* for their sounds. It is a miracle that they find any responsive readers at all, so incessant has been the pedagogical pressure, over fifty years, not to let "the music" take you until you have first secured the sense.

We say of these rhythms—large scale and small scale alike—that they "ride through," not that they "bind together." Perhaps that sort of binding, and that sort of boundedness, are among the things that the poem would warn us against, and advise us not to expect. But how would it be, if we were to say that none of them "come home" to us? That seems to be what is said by the last lines quoted from *Briggflatts*, and by *Briggflatts* as a whole:

> *It looks well on the page, but never*
> *well enough. Something is lost*
> *when wind, sun, sea upbraid*
> *justly an unconvinced deserter.*

After a professional lifetime of strenuous apprenticeship to Poundian precepts and models, Basil Bunting came into his own only in his sixties, when at last he brought all of his acquired skills and responsiveness to bear on his native Northumberland. Pound may be thought to have warned Bunting that that was how it would have to be, when he represented Bunting in *Confucius to Cummings* (1964) by two of his most Northumbrian and least overtly Poundian poems. It is what we might expect of the poet who told Hardy, "I come from an American suburb. . . . The suburb has no roots, no centre of life"; who wrote in *The New Age* in 1920, "I was brought up in a district or city with which my forebears had no connection and I am therefore accustomed to being alien in one place or another";[5] who had written, moreover, in *Patria Mia*, "the person whom it is the fashion to call 'sentimentalist,' does not emigrate. I mean the person who has 'the finer feelings,' love of home, love of land, love of place. . . ." If this was indeed Pound's trouble, he was the first to diagnose it; and it is remarkable that those who are readiest to declare themselves his debtors have all very deliberately invested their sentiments in some one place—William Carlos Williams in Paterson, New Jersey; Charles Olson in Gloucester, Massachusetts; Basil Bunting in Northumbria. It will be recalled that the epithet Pound found for his anti-Semitism, when he repudiated it, was "suburban."

The only reason why we cannot scan the lines from Canto 47 (our second excerpt) is that we haven't an adequate system of notation, and any that we might devise would have to be too cumbrous to be useful. The traditional notation—if it is properly used and understood, as it very seldom is, for the entire science of traditional prosody has been willfully thrown away—very ingeniously accounts for two distinct principles that govern meter in the vastly greater part of poetry in English since the mid-sixteenth century: accent (or stress, or "beat," or *ictus*) on the one hand, syllable counting on the other. This notation will reveal that of the twenty-four lines given from Canto 47, no less than eighteen can be scanned as anapaestic trimeter, though (as in Jonson's poem) continually varied with reversed feet and substitutions. Since, as we saw, this is the dominant meter in Jonson's poem also, it was presumably by establishing it so firmly that Pound was able to allude to Jonson so smoothly.

To scan the passage thus is a great deal better than nothing, and there is no excuse for our doing it so seldom. Yet such scansion leaves out of account entirely another principle that operates in all English verse for good or ill: the principle of *quantity*, of duration, of length of syllable—a principle which becomes more and more important as the English verse we examine becomes verse for singing rather than speaking. Pound would say that traditional prosody is as helpless before this dimension of Jonson's "metrical" verse as before the supposedly "nonmetrical" verse of the *Cantos*; and Pound would be right.

The excerpts from the later Cantos show Pound exploiting, with the resources of modern typesetting to help him, yet another principle or element of English verse for which we have no notation, nor can expect to find any—what he had called "government of speed." Pace and tempo, acceleration or retardation of the speaking or singing voice—this is what Pound seeks to register (and does, for the sensitive reader) in his use of deep or shallow typographical indentations, in dropping from one printed line to the next, in the leaving blank of typographical spaces within the line, and in the use of the diagonal bar on the typewriter.

However, the excerpt from Canto 81—which Pound in the margin marked as *"libretto"*—is a tour de force which deserves special attention. Here Pound has to maneuver his verse so as to incorporate, not just the by now familiar anapaestic trimeters of Jonson, but also, as soon as possible afterwards, the iambic pentameters of Chaucer. How he does it is a joy to contemplate. He begins with trochaic tetrameters:

> *Ere the season died a-cold*
>
> *Borne upon a zephyr's shoulder*

Then, using the extra unstressed syllable (the "-er" of "shoulder"), he is able to modulate smoothly into the rising trimeter,

> *I rose through the aureate sky*

—which brings him at once within range of the anapaestic trimeters of Jonson, so securely indeed that he can afford to revert to trochaic tetrameters for his refrain:

> *Lawes and Jenkyns guard thy rest*
>
> *Dolmetsch ever be thy guest . . .*

The next three lines give us the anapaestic or rising trimeter, deliciously unabashed (the second line calling on the typesetter to make the intention unmistakable):

> *Has he tempered the viol's wood*
>
> *To enforce   both the grave   and the acute?*
>
> *Has he curved us the bowl of the lute?*

After a return to the solid tetrameters of the refrain (as I've remarked, this alternation between disyllabic and trisyllabic measures is a structural principle of the Jonson original), we have rising trimeters again, alluding to Jonson not just in meter but in diction also:

Hast 'ou fashioned so airy a mood

    To draw up leaf from the root?

Hast 'ou found   a cloud   so light
As seemed neither mist nor shade?

But by this time the allusion to Chaucer is already in the offing, and Pound has to begin working toward it. He does so by gradually, and yet rapidly, shortening his rising measure from trisyllabic to disyllabic (from "anapaestic" to "iambic"), in the third of the lines just quoted calling on the typesetter to make it plain that this is what he is doing. I have not subjected the last line to any metrical notation—and for a very good reason, for this line is metrically quite ambiguous, and the contrived ambiguity is crucial to the transition that Pound is intent on making—to the iambic pentameters of Chaucer. If we read "as seemèd"—the archaic diction of the preceding lines having given us ample warrant for such an archaism—the line comes out as solid tetrameter in rising (iambic) measure:

As seemed neither mist nor shade . . .

Yet if we read "seem'd," the line is rising trimeter, in line with what has preceded it:

As seemed neither mist nor shade.

For what it is worth, in performance I prefer to implement the first possibility, rising tetrameter, since this provides the smoothest transition to the refrain which (we now find—surprise, surprise!) has reversed itself from a falling into a rising measure:

> *Then resolve me, tell me aright*
>
> *If Waller sang or Dowland played . . .*

The first of these lines still permits a trisyllabic foot; the second is throughout disyllabic (iambic). And from iambic tetrameter thus arrived at, it is child's play to lengthen the measure into Chaucer's pentameters:

> *Your eyen two wol sleye me sodenly*
> *I may the beauté of hem nat susteyne.*

In English there is no other poet of the twentieth century, and few of any century, with an ear fine enough to have managed this progression. And in demonstrating it we've taken note only of those principles which our notation can register. The haunting musicality depends equally on other principles at work, which we detect at work but have no way of registering.

Toward a Conclusion

vi

John Masefield, in his memoir *So Long to Learn*, wrote of himself as one "who belonged to a literary time, when all read much, and often found the delightful spoil of so much reading a hindrance when they came to tell a tale." Masefield is right, of course, as was Paul Verlaine when in the same literary time he exhorted his fellows to "take literature and wring its neck." The literariness choked or sapped many literary talents of that time—Maurice Hewlett's, Masefield's own, R. L. Stevenson's, many another. Pound may stand as the greatest example of how a stubborn talent could force its way through that underbrush. For Pound was more bookish than any of them. And yet he lived to prove, by his best writings, that a passion for past literature, if it sometimes grows up into strangling entanglements, can also bear sustaining fruit. A book like the *ABC of Reading* suggests further that this state of affairs is normal; that literature has always fed—not exclusively of course, but crucially—on its own past. Pound's career shows that it can do so still, that it *must* do so, that there is no alternative—or so we may suppose, noting in Pound's lifetime the false alternatives of several "metapoetries" which have ended in silence, having destroyed the poetry that they thought to go "beyond." And Pound's slogan, "Make It New," affords little comfort to the avant-garde; it is a recipe for conservation, for protecting past monuments in all their potency.

Pound's significance, for those who are not principally concerned for poetry, his or any other, may be thought to turn therefore on what we understand by "a literary civilization"; whether we want any more of it; and, supposing we do, what chance we stand of getting it in any future that we can foresee.

In the first place, such a civilization will have as its avowed end, quite unashamedly, *pleasure*—John Masefield's "delightful spoil." Literature may instruct, and the poet of *The Cantos* certainly acted in the belief that it did; but if it instructs, it instructs only by pleasing—surreptitiously, through the delights that it brings. Moreover, if we trust Pound, the pleasure that literature brings is direct and as if immediate, like the pleasure of cool air brushing against one's bared and heated skin. This depends upon a sensuous aliveness in ourselves such as Pound had when he spoke of the "effect of a decent climate where a man leaves his nerve-set open, or allows it to tune into its ambience." To such a sensuous awareness the other arts—sculpture, architecture, painting, music, the dance—are sources of pleasure and of whatever instruction that pleasure brings with it, just as literature is. Accordingly, in a literary civilization the civilized man is first and foremost he who can discriminate among pleasures; he is in fact the *dilettante*—a word that needs to be cleaned of the mud that stuck to it as soon as it was adopted from Romance languages into English; that is to say, from cultures which put a high value on sensuous pleasure, into the Anglophone cultures which feared or hated it. To Pound it seemed, as it has to others, that in Protestant cultures it was the Hebraic component which instilled fear and distrust of sensuous pleasure; and so he threw his weight always on the side of the Hellenic voice which called on sculptors to make images of the gods, as against the Hebraic iconoclasm which was set against "graven images." To Pound we may concede that a literary civilization does not *have to* elevate literature above the sister arts, though it is apparent that in the Anglophone nations it often has.

However, the pleasures of literature cannot be *logically* of the same order with the pleasures of the senses. Indeed, literature differs from the other arts in not appealing, immediately, to any of the senses whatsoever. And to minds of a certain (very un-Poundian) sort, that is in fact an argument for the pre-eminence of literature among the arts: that all its pleasures are mental. But to this there is, in any case, one partial but momentous exception: poetry composed so as to be spoken aloud, or to be chanted or sung to a suitably scrupulous accompaniment, *does* address itself directly to one of the senses. It addresses itself directly to the ear, by creating discernible and pleasurable audible rhythms. And this, as one might expect, is a dimension of literature with which Pound concerned himself very assiduously throughout his career. (It explains, for instance, why in Pound's pantheon Edmund Waller the songwriter occupies a place more appropriately given, one might think, to Donne or Milton, Pope or Dryden.) Nothing marks Pound off so sharply from the avant-garde of the past thirty years, which tries to sail under his colors; for this avant-garde, if it does not explicitly abandon audible rhythms in poetry as a traditional indulgence which it will no longer tolerate, concerns itself with them not at all so as to give pleasure to reader or auditor but on the contrary only so as to stay purportedly more true to the mood, and the sensitive or even physical constitution, of the poet. It was not thus, nor on those grounds, that Pound declared: "To break the pentameter, that was the first heave." It was not that Pound thought he could not be "true to himself" in the pentameter; if at a certain stage he wanted to "break the pentameter"—that is to say, to destroy in his own ear and the ear of his reader the expectations which that Shakespearean meter had created over one literary generation after another—it was because Pound knew himself capable of creating for his reader rhythmical pleasures which the expectation of the pentameter prevented both him and his reader from realizing. Many critics who would deny to Pound any other achievement have allowed him at least this one—that he had "an ear," that he truly could command a range of audible rhythms which only a liberation from the authority of the pentameter permitted him first, and his reader afterward, to recognize, positively *to hear*.

We come back to the important point that, with the crucial if partial exception just noted, the senses cannot be pleasured by literature at all so directly as the eye by painting, the ear by music, the senses of sight and touch by sculpture, and so on. This is a crucial consideration for the notion of a literary civilization, though the crux is seldom recognized. Literature can and does create the fantasy or the illusion of direct experience through the eye, the ear, the fingertips; and this means that the notion of a perception can be, thanks to the graces and powers of language, at least as powerful and convincing as the perception itself. This phenomenon, which can be directly experienced by all except that unfortunate few who are tone-deaf to literature as others are to music, exposes the sterility of all those lines of argument (espoused by the avant-garde as often as by its paste-board antagonist, "the bourgeois philistine"), which start, as Plato did, from the supposition that through literature we experience actuality only "at one remove." The "remove" which language represents is so integral with human nature—the human creature being above all that creature who *speaks*—that to speak of it as "a remove" is already to betray our humanity.

First, then, a literary civilization is focused on pleasure; second, the pleasure in question is experienced as sensuously immediate, for all that it is in fact mediated through language. A momentous possibility arises: since sense perceptions conceptualized in language can thus be experienced as if they were immediate, may not concepts be substantialized in language so that they can be experienced immediately, as if they were perceptions? Of course they can. The whole of *The Divine Comedy* is a witness to this capacity of the human imagination operating through language. Dante's poem has to be a sacred object for any literary civilization, as it was for Pound and for his peers and co-workers T. S. Eliot and W. B. Yeats. Perhaps for them, as for us and our children in any foreseeable future, it has to be *the* central object, the ark of the literary covenant, as, for instance, Shakespeare's plays or Homer's epics are not —and this not because those literary monuments are less "great," but because they are not focused so consistently as Dante's is on this particular capacity of human language, the corporealizing of *idea*, the transforming of the notional into something apprehensible, or *as if* apprehensible, through the senses. The effect of this is to bring concepts—such as Justice or Candor or Clarity, Injustice or Double-dealing or Confusion—under the same rule of pleasure (and, necessarily, pain) as rules over sense perceptions. Literature mediates for us with the world of ideas, just as it does with the world of sight and sound, taste and smell; indeed, it traffics both ways with such a shuttle service that we find ourselves wanting to say, and able to say, of such and such an idea that it is "luminous," of such and such another that it "smells fishy." And so we are made free of a world in which strenuous intellection—for instance, the constructing or the following of a close argument—affords a pleasure of precisely the same order as lovemaking or a well-fought tennis match. This possibility appears to have been what excited the troubadours of medieval Provence, especially in relation to the concept which they called "AMOR," as it excited also the poets of the *dolce stil nuovo* who learned from them. Pound was compelled to recognize the possibility as soon as he studied Arnaud Daniel and Dante's predecessors and

Dante himself; and from the chapters in *The Spirit of Romance* which he devoted to these masters, through to the last verses he ever wrote, Pound was exploring and realizing this possibility.

He explored it not as a specialist or a *savant*, but as a lover. And how the lover responds to the beloved is something that we think we know about, though whatever we know is thanks to the troubadours. The lover, we suppose, seeks to possess the beloved, but in a way that makes possession different from appropriation. (Don Juan, on the other hand, is every inch a professional, an expert, a specialist, as it were a *scholar*.) When Dante in Canto III of the *Paradiso* substantiates his idea of the lunar spirits by writing—

> *In such guise as, from glasses transparent and polished, or from waters clear and tranquil, not so deep that the bottom is darkened,*
> *come back the notes of our faces, so faint that a pearl on a white brow cometh not slowlier, upon our pupils;*
> *so did I behold many a countenance, eager to speak . . .*

—the professional, the Dante scholar, will find many proper and honorable things to do with the passage, all of them tainted however with appropriation. The amateur, under the simple impulsion of pleasure, of delight, seeks only one object, possession. If he is Laurence Binyon he will possess the passage by retranslating it, with Pound's enthusiastic encouragement, into an idiom more genuinely his than the Rossettian language that Pound was content with when he gave the passage thus in *The Spirit of Romance*. If the amateur is Pound, he may wait for forty years until he can write—

And that your eyes come to the surface
  from the deep wherein they were sunken,

(CANTO 91)

and

Light & the flowing crystal
  never gin in cut glass had such clarity
That Drake saw the splendour and wreckage
    in that clarity
Gods moving in crystal.

(CANTO 91)

—which is re-translation also, in its way. It is reverent emulation. And as for the amateur who has no skill with words, he can presumably still possess the Dante by schooling himself, with such a passage for model, to let his perceptions and his ideas interact on a common plane, as Dante's do.

A sneer at the academy is always in order. All the same, for reasons we've just glanced at, it is certain that the institution of a new professorship in Romance philology, or the graduation of a class of some hundreds who have "majored" in English or American literature, does little or nothing to bring nearer, or to keep in being, a literary civilization of the sort we're talking about. About this, Pound was not very clairvoyant. On the contrary, one of the many threads of pathos in Pound's life derives from the fact that, far more than any of his peers, he responded to what he called "the romance of scholarship," gratefully cooperated with and learned from scholars, and acknowledged the worth of the scholarly enterprise; and yet scholars have hounded him, and hound him still, as they have never hounded his friend who wrote:

All shuffle there; all cough in ink;
All wear the carpet with their shoes;
All think what other people think;
All know the man their neighbour knows.

Yeats's "The Scholars" is a cheap because sweeping gibe, such as Pound never stooped to. The reason is that Yeats's education never brought him within smelling distance of what scholarly scruple and discipline really are, whereas Pound was a thoroughly trained scholar in his own field before ever he came to Europe. Just that, it seems, is what the scholars cannot forgive him: having "his own field" (the note of appropriation is unmistakable), he was too inquisitive and eager to stay inside it. It is out of this conception of the world of learning as parceled out into so many fenced "fields," each jealously guarded by the certified experts who alone have grazing rights within it, that there comes the voice which says: "Behind everything that Pound wrote is a hideous set of delusions, that he understood Greek, Latin and Chinese. . . ."[1] Pound was *not* deluded; he *did* understand these languages, as well as any of us can hope to understand them if we are not professional Latinists, Hellenists, Sinologists. We have the right to stray in those pastures, without having to flash a certificate at the gate. Pound most vehemently in his generation claimed that right on our behalf. To some scholars, such presumption is "hideous," but a literary civilization depends on our having that right, and we have a duty to enforce it. The scholar has the right and the duty to correct our howlers; we are in duty bound to do our best

[1] "Fragments of Cracker," *Times Literary Supplement* (March 16, 1973).

to avoid them, but we have the right to make them, as of course we shall.

None of this is out of keeping with the first tentative "fix" that we took on Pound and the position he occupies; that is to say, the Edwardian man of letters. It is since George Saintsbury's time that the territories which Saintsbury roamed through as an omnivorous amateur have been carved up into scholars' preserves, professionalized, industrialized. Pound's focus, moreover, like Saintsbury's, was on the Mediterranean, though he demanded and asserted the right to move out from that center as far as the ripples of cultural history might take him. Beside and behind Rome, Greece; and behind archaic Greece, ancient Egypt—though Pound got access to that only late, through his son-in-law, Boris de Rachewiltz. Similarly, when he began to interest himself in African cultures, it was in the steps of the German archaeologist Leo Frobenius, who had proved, or thought he had proved, that the West African cultures he was investigating had been in constant contact with the Greek city-states, by Aegean ships on the sea passage past the Pillars of Hercules.

To this Mediterranean-centered concern there appears to be one glaring exception: Pound's interest in Chinese. But as Hugh Kenner in particular has shown, Pound's concern with Chinese was initially, and for a long time, Europe-centered. It was an interest like that of Voltaire and Goldsmith and other amateurs of the Enlightenment; learning from Jesuit missionaries the features of this civilization which had developed on the other side of the world in almost total isolation from their own, these Europeans eagerly attended to reports from China so as to find confirmation of their hunch, or their conviction, that human nature was always and everywhere basically the same. Even when Pound, in *Guide to Kulchur*, decided that the Chinese Confucian tradition was a surer guide in ethics and civics than the Aristotelian Greek, he was still just within the world of Enlightenment *chinoiserie*. However, in his last fifteen years, when he was enthusiastic for the Na-Khi (non-Chinese) civilization of southwest China, he had certainly broken away from any controlling European center. By that time it was clear that he had grievously misconstrued the relationship between Confucianism and the Tao in Chinese culture; and he was also plunging at the heels of various cranks and charlatans into the prehistory of Babylon and other cultures of the Middle East. He had lost his direction, and his Mediterranean anchorage. "The centre cannot hold," Yeats had said in desperation. And from about 1955, it was no longer holding for Pound. We can feel the anchor beginning to drag in the 1930s and 1940s, then it grips again for perhaps ten years after the shock and torment of Pisa in 1945, and then it lets go again. So long as it holds, it holds to the seabed of the Aegean.

After all, for a literary civilization that English-speakers can be part of, where else can the anchorage be? This is a reactionary sentiment indeed! On all sides it is urged upon us that for salvation and certainty we must look elsewhere than to the two Aegean cultures, Greek and Hebrew, which, as codified by Roman law, came together to make historic Christendom. And certainly what can we feel but dismay at the world which two thousand years of Christendom have left us with? We do well to look elsewhere, and to wonder if two millennia of Zen Buddhism, or even Siberian shamanism, might not have delivered us a world more habitable and less patently unjust. It is thus that we are compelled to look and to wonder by Pound's Confucianism when it is at its most eloquent and compelling, as in his translation of the Confucian classic which he came around to calling *The Unwobbling Pivot* (1947). We can do more than look and wonder, we can learn from such alternatives. But all the same they are not alternatives in the here-and-now. They are wistful might-have-beens. If the world we have inherited had been formed by Buddhism or Confucianism, then it would have been a very different world, and quite possibly a better one. But the world is not our oyster, and we are not free to pick and choose in it. Like it or not, the world we have been born to was formed by Christendom and cradled in the Mediterranean. To the Edwardians this seemed self-evident; what is important about Pound's writings as an intellectual force and witness is that he hung on to this conviction during a period when it became less and less self-evident, when, on the contrary, more and more people came to think that this inherited culture had shown itself bankrupt.

We have already remarked that to a mind of this temper the Italian Mussolini would be a beguiling figure, as the Russian Stalin or the German Hitler was not. But there are other ways of relating Pound's cultural and imaginative proclivities with his political aberrations. We know so little about how political predispositions are formed that any number of explanations are possible, and there is no way of adjudicating among them. But one such explanation might start from a consideration that *this* Edwardian was American, and very conscious of it. For Pound seems to have regarded

Mussolini through many years as an "enlightened despot," like the Archduke Leopold of Tuscany, whom he never tired of applauding as the founder of a just bank, the Monte dei Paschi of Siena. That curious phase in the political history of Europe, the "age of enlightened despotism," is a manifestation of that eighteenth-century Enlightenment culture to which, as we have seen, Pound was eagerly responsive—especially when, relatively late in his life, he came to see the United States, as framed in its Constitution and conducted by the Founding Fathers, as itself a product of the Enlightenment. Thus, although at times Pound's attitude to Mussolini seems not unlike Voltaire's to Frederick the Great or Diderot's to Catherine of Russia, his allegiance becomes dangerously more wholehearted than theirs because his identity and loyalty as an American are enlisted in support of it.[2] Something of this sort lies behind his *Jefferson and/or Mussolini* (1935), as behind his disastrous wartime broadcasts from Rome.

To support this anachronistic reading of the political scene of the 1930s and 1940s, Pound could draw upon another component of his American heritage besides the constitutional America of Jefferson and Adams, and apart from the intellectual America of Boston, New York, and Philadelphia, which he shared with Henry James and Eliot. Another America, which Pound knew only at second hand through his father and grand-

[2] Upward had written in 1908, of "the backwash of the great French Revolution," "The educated European mind has been marking time for a hundred years, out of fear of the mob. Frederick of Prussia, Catherine of Russia . . . were . . . more enlightened than kings have ventured to be since." (*The New Word*, Twentieth Head.)

father, also impelled him toward the Fascist solution. This was the small-town frontier America which had produced William Jennings Bryan, an America which had already made its presence felt in Pound's confidently impatient pronouncements on fiscal and monetary matters, and even (it may be) in his anti-Semitism. This was an America which trusted the pronouncements of the plain man and the cracker-barrel philosopher, and which believed—as perhaps it still believes— that diagnosis and cure alike can be pithily expressed in a few sentences and words of one syllable, if only one cuts through the sophistications and refinements of the big-city intellectuals. This proclivity too, oddly enough, could find itself vindicated in the Age of Enlightened Despotism; for characteristic of that age was a faith in "the virtue of formulas and the efficacy of axioms," and a belief that the ideal political constitution "could be set forth, at least in plan and outline, on a small sheet of paper."[3] This is very strikingly true of Pound's political thinking, and his Confucianism only strengthened this predisposition toward maxim and apothegm and the "small sheet of paper." Indeed, the Confucius of the *Analects*, as Pound translates him, is very much the small-town wiseacre, the cracker-barrel sage. The least one can say is that fascism appealed to the Pound who was American by birth as to the Pound who was European by adoption. It has, in any event, on this showing, nothing to do with his being "literary"; and so Pound's case by itself gives no warrant for concluding, as some have done, that fascism is a political false solution that

[3] Albert Sorel, *Europe and the French Revolution* (1885), tr. A. Cobban and J. W. Hunt (New York, 1969), p. 148.

twentieth-century literary men are particularly prone to. Much more might be said, and needs to be said, about what a literary civilization might be, as we find it partly adumbrated, partly taken for granted, by Pound. But we're already at a point where we can ask what hope there is of such a civilization being realized in any world that we can foresee.

In the first place, for such a civilization to be based on the principle of pleasure does not commit it to a vulgar hedonism. That a literary civilization will be focused on pleasure, and on sensuous pleasure as the touchstone or paradigm of other pleasures allegedly "higher," does not mean that there are not pleasures available to us which are vicious and must be abjured. As late as 1935, by which time Pound's prose had already become brutal and rabble-rousing, he began a review of John Buchan's *Oliver Cromwell*: "By great wisdom sodomy and usury were seen coupled together."[4] And he meant to shock his readers by the suggestion that usury was as vicious as sodomy. But how quaintly this reads, now in 1976, when sodomy may be taken by the enlightened as just one of the sexual pleasures indiscriminately available to us! A young reader who has been introduced to this and similar notions of "the sexual revolution" may well be puzzled by that favorite of the anthologists, Canto 45:

> *Usura rusteth the chisel*
> *It rusteth the craft and the craftsman*
> *It gnaweth the thread in the loom*
> *None learneth to weave gold in her pattern;*

[4] *Ezra Pound: Selected Prose, 1909–1965*, William Cookson, ed. (New York, 1973), p. 265; reprinted from *The New English Weekly* (June 6, 1935).

> *Azure hath a canker by usura; cramoisi is unbroidered*
> *Emerald findeth no Memling*
> *Usura slayeth the child in the womb*
> *It stayeth the young man's courting*
> *It hath brought palsey to bed, lyeth*
> *between the young bride and her bridegroom*
>
> CONTRA NATURAM
>
> *They have brought whores for Eleusis*
> *Corpses are set to banquet*
> *at behest of usura.*

Rightly detecting that Pound is here fulminating against contraception as bleakly as any Roman theologian, readers who have grown up among ecological slogans ("The Population Explosion Is Everybody's Baby!") will have no difficulty recognizing how conservative he is. They will think him a moralist so conservative that he can only be disregarded.

But if they reach that conclusion about Pound, of how many other poets must they not decide the same? This is little recognized; there is no connection, we suppose, between the practice of the arts and the practice, or nonpractice, of birth control. But as long as, talking of the arts, we make use of the crucial pun on "conception" and "conceive," (as of the analogous puns or metaphors folded into words like "seminal" and "disseminate," "brooding" and "pregnant," and many another), so long in fact as we want to hold by the ancient claim for artistic creation that it reveres the Natural Creation by emulating it—it is clear that the arts are directly menaced by every piece of propaganda for family planning or voluntary sterilization. The humanitarian motives behind such propaganda need not be questioned. We may even concede, for the sake of argument, that it is both right and necessary. But if it is so, then any literary civilization which acknowledges that right and that necessity can persist only in a spirit very different from any that has informed literary civilizations of the past—a spirit so different indeed that to give it the same name is positively deceitful. This is an instance of how, through a long period when literary men have been squaring up to threats supposedly posed to them by the physicist and the chemist, the truly baleful threats have come—as they come still—from the "soft" sciences of the behaviorist, the demographer, and the statistician.

The pleasures of making love, so the churches have told us, are distinct from the pleasures of propagating children. Whereas the churches in the past supposed that propagation was a higher pleasure than copulation, we now see emerging a morality in which the old "higher" and "lower" must change places (though the very word "copulation" trips us up even so). What is common to the supposedly discredited morality and the emergent one is the supposition that there is a hierarchy of pleasures, by which some are "higher"—more responsible or more refined, not just more *intense*—than others. Neither morality can accept the Rabelaisian "*Fay ce que tu vouldras*." And so there is nothing super-annuated about Pound's Dantesque and conservative assumption that our pleasures can and must be ranged on a scale of relative value, in which for instance the pleasures of usury and buggery may be on a par, and so low in the scale that we must call them vicious. That particular ranking may be questioned, but not the assumption that ranking of some kind there must be.

From a hierarchy of pleasures it is a short step to a

hierarchy of classes. In the recent past the stepping-stone was the proposition that for the savoring of certain pleasures—notably, those offered by many works of art—there was need of *leisure*, a commodity which in the nature of things only a privileged minority could afford. But modern technological societies, though they are still very far from securing adequate leisure for us all, seem on the way to doing so. And a stronger case now might rest on the proposition that certain pleasures call for privacy and silence, or at least for *quiet*—this last being rather plainly a commodity which is rarer as leisure becomes more widely shared. However that may be, there can be no doubt that Pound *did* believe in a social hierarchy, as we may suspect any enthusiast for a literary civilization must. Yet, one may believe in the necessity for such a hierarchy without requiring that it be overt and institutionalized in explicitly accorded social and economic privileges; and whereas Eliot by the time he wrote *Notes Toward the Definition of Culture* (1949) seems to have decided that the hierarchy must be thus overt, Pound—always a poor man, a maverick, and a bohemian—thought rather of the hierarchy as spiritual and arcane, its highest rank a secret brotherhood of initiates who recognized each other by signs that outsiders did not know about. It is in this spirit that he records with gratification Henry James saying to him, "And there is another inner and more secret body, eh, doubtless you belong to it. . . ."[5] In Pound's view this secret *élite* can take care of itself; it composes and decomposes and recomposes itself, in every generation. All he asks, at least for himself and

---

[5] *Der Querschnitt* (Berlin, 1924). I owe this reference to John Peck.

his peers, is to be left alone. It is a lot to ask, and more than any of us are likely to get. And so if Pound was right in thinking it a prerequisite for a literary civilization, on those grounds too the chances for such a civilization are not good.

CONCLUSION

A reviewer of Noel Stock's *Life of Ezra Pound*, William Chace, found in that biography "no description or explanation of the inwardness of Pound, the man behind the letters, projects, discoveries, hatreds, obsessions, and spectacular literary talent." And this, so Chace thought, came about not through any deficiency in the biographer but "because the Pound *within* the great vortex of energy and creation does not exist." Neither from Stock nor anyone else could Chace get answers to his questions: "Why did this happen? What did Pound then feel? Was this emotionally a challenge or that a disappointment to him?"[1]

This is surely excessive. There are the two letters to Hardy; and there was apparently, in 1950, a letter of hurt protest to Wyndham Lewis which we know about

[1] *The Southern Review* (January, 1972), pp. 232–33.

from Lewis's reply.[2] More to the point, there is *Discretions* by Pound's daughter, Mary de Rachewiltz, from which there emerges a figure almost stately, with old-fashioned and unrelenting views about what a father might demand of his child. (He might, for instance, set her to learning English by translating *Under the Greenwood Tree* into Italian.) *Discretions*, a very remarkable book written out of hard-earned affection and profound but not starry-eyed respect, suggests strongly that it was not only the young Pound who "put up a front" to the world; in particular, that the extraordinary style of Pound's letters (to some a delight, to others an exasperation) was a prolongation to the end of his life of the weirdly fabricated social *persona* which people found so disconcerting in the programmatic decade. A mask worn for so long grows onto the face beneath. And yet Pound in the end could throw it off; that is the meaning, surely, of the tersely self-disgusted recantations and disavowals of his last years, in moving verse as well as in conversation. Thus there *was* a face behind the mask, and a person within the vortex. It is an elusive person, certainly. But is it any more elusive than other persons who are equally given up to, and dispersed in, the energies of their language? One thinks of Dryden, particularly one thinks (incautiously) of Shakespeare. Keats in a famous letter called the phenomenon "negative capability." Pound, if he had this capability, sometimes distrusted it; often it is as if Shakespeare tried to behave like Ben Jonson, or Dryden tried to make himself over into Milton. This is true of

[2] *The Letters of Wyndham Lewis*, W. K. Rose, ed. (New York, 1963), p. 517.

Pound in his social relations; it is less often true, but still too often for comfort, of the Pound who wrote poems. Nevertheless, Dryden and Keats and, yes, Shakespeare are the appropriate fellows for this poet of our time who magnanimously lent his energies to the language that we all share, rather than bending that language to his own egotistical purposes. Pound as a young man foresaw that fate for himself, and gloried in it:

> Search not my lips, O Love, let go my hands,
> This thing that moves as man is no more mortal.
> If thou hast seen my shade sans character,
> If thou hast seen that mirror of all moments,
> That glass to all things that o'ershadow it,
> Call not that mirror me, for I have slipped
> Your grasp, I have eluded.

SHORT BIBLIOGRAPHY

Principal Works of Pound

POEMS

A Lume Spento, 1908; reissued, 1965.
Canzoni, 1909.
Personae, 1909.

  (The same title was given, confusingly, to a volume of 1926, *Personae. The Collected Poems of Ezra Pound*, which was really a "Selected Shorter Poems," including both *Hugh Selwyn Mauberley* and *Homage to Sextus Propertius*. With two appendices presenting additional material, this was reissued in 1949 and 1952 as *Personae: Collected Shorter Poems of Ezra Pound*. This last, now available in paperback, is all that most readers will need for Pound's poetry outside of *The Cantos*.)

Ripostes, 1912.
Lustra, 1916.
Quia Pauper Amavi, 1919 (including *Homage to Sextus Propertius*, and drafts of the first three *Cantos*, later canceled).

Hugh Selwyn Mauberley, 1920.
A Draft of XXX Cantos, 1930.
Eleven New Cantos, 1934.
The Fifth Decad of Cantos, 1937.
Cantos LII–LXXI, 1940.
The Pisan Cantos, 1948.
Section Rock-Drill: 85–95 de los Cantares, 1955.
Thrones: 96–109 de los Cantares, 1959.
Drafts and Fragments of Cantos CX–CXVII, 1969.
The Cantos of Ezra Pound (1–117), 1970.
  (The *Selected Cantos*, though Pound made the selection,
  is unsatisfactory; a better selection from *The Cantos* is in
  Ezra Pound: Selected Poems. New York: New Directions
  paperback, 1957.)

TRANSLATIONS

   This category is misleading: the frontier between translation and original composition was fruitfully blurred for
Pound throughout his career; and important translations
can be found in all his books of poetry and most of his
prose books also.

Sonnets and Ballate of Guido Cavalcanti, 1912.
Cathay, 1915.
Noh, or Accomplishment, 1916 (stylized plays, from the
  Japanese).
The Natural Philosophy of Love, by Remy de Gourmont,
  1922.
Confucius: The Unwobbling Pivot, and *The Great Digest*,
  1947; with *The Analects*, 1969.
Women of Trachis, 1956 (verse-tragedy, from the Greek of
  Sophocles).
The Classic Anthology Defined by Confucius, 1954 (ancient
  Chinese poems).
   See also Hugh Kenner, ed., *The Translations of Ezra
Pound*, 1953 (enlarged edition; New York: New Direc-
tions, 1963).

PROSE

The Spirit of Romance, 1910 (reissued and valuably en-
  larged, 1952).
Gaudier-Brzeska: A Memoir, 1916 (reissued, 1960).
Instigations, 1920.
ABC of Reading, 1934.
Make It New, 1934.
Jefferson and/or Mussolini, 1935.
Polite Essays, 1937.
Guide to Kulchur (in the U.S. *Culture*), 1938.
  As the title suggests, *ABC of Reading* is probably where to
  start; and *The Spirit of Romance* comes next. Note also
  The Literary Essays of Ezra Pound, T. S. Eliot, ed., 1954;
  and *Ezra Pound: Selected Prose 1909–1965*, William
  Cookson, ed., New York: New Directions, 1973.

ANTHOLOGIES

Catholic Anthology, 1914–1915, 1915.
Active Anthology, 1933.
Confucius to Cummings (with Marcella Spann), 1964.

LETTERS

The Letters of Ezra Pound, 1907–1941. D. D. Paige, ed. New
  York: Harcourt Brace, 1950.
Pound/Joyce. *The Letters of Ezra Pound to James Joyce,
  with Pound's Essays on Joyce*. Forrest Read, ed. New
  York: New Directions, 1965.

BIBLIOGRAPHY

Gallup, Donald. *A Bibliography of Ezra Pound*. New York:
  Oxford University Press, 1964.

Books about Pound

BIOGRAPHY

Norman, Charles. *Ezra Pound: A Biography*. New York: Macmillan, 1960 (reissued 1969).
Stock, Noel. *The Life of Ezra Pound*. New York: Pantheon Books, 1970.

EXPOSITION AND CRITICISM

Anything before the truly pioneering study, Hugh Kenner's *The Poetry of Ezra Pound* (New York: New Directions, 1951), is of mostly historical interest; and that book in turn is superseded by Kenner's massive and masterly, though still partisan, *The Pound Era* (Berkeley: University of California Press, 1971). Slighter and more manageable introductory studies are by G. S. Fraser, *Ezra Pound* (New York: Grove Press, 1961); and by M. L. Rosenthal, *A Primer of Ezra Pound* (New York: Macmillan, 1960). More extended attempts to scrutinize Pound's writings as a whole are by G. G. Dekker, *The Cantos of Ezra Pound: A Critical Study* (New York: Barnes & Noble, 1963); and by D. Davie, *Ezra Pound: Poet as Sculptor* (New York: Oxford University Press, 1964).
Books on particular phases of Pound's long career are:
Dembo, L. S. *The Confucian Odes of Ezra Pound: A Critical Appraisal*. Berkeley: University of California Press, 1963.
Espey, John J. *Ezra Pound's Mauberley: A Study in Composition*. Berkeley: University of California Press, 1955.
Schneidau, Herbert N. *Ezra Pound: The Image and the Real*. Baton Rouge: Louisiana State University Press, 1969.
Sullivan, J. P. *Ezra Pound and Sextus Propertius: A Study in Creative Translation*. Austin: University of Texas Press, 1964.
Witemeyer, Hugh. *The Poetry of Ezra Pound: Forms and Renewal, 1908–20*. Berkeley: University of California Press, 1969.

On the *Cantos* specifically, see:

Edwards, John H., and Vasse, William W., Jr. *Annotated Index to the Cantos of Ezra Pound.* Berkeley: University of California Press, 1957 (which necessarily gives no help with later *Cantos*).

Emery, Clark M. *Ideas into Action: A Study of Pound's Cantos.* Coral Gables: University of Miami Press, 1959.

Leary, Lewis, ed. *Motive and Method in the Cantos of Ezra Pound.* New York: Columbia University Press, 1961.

Pearlman, Daniel D. *The Barb of Time; on the Unity of Pound's Cantos.* New York: Oxford University Press, 1969.

An invaluable selection from criticism of Pound over sixty years is *Ezra Pound.* Penguin Critical Anthology, J. P. Sullivan, ed. (1970). For exhaustive and sometimes sterile explication of particular difficulties, see *Agenda* (U.K.) and *Paideuma* (U.S.), recent and current issues.

INDEX

A Lume Spento, xi, 2 15
ABC of Reading, 88, 92, 100
Adams, John Q., 8, 25, 111
Aeschylus, 90
Agassiz, Louis, 66n
"Allen Upward and Ezra
    Pound" (Knox), 42n
"Allen Upward Serious," 72n
Ambassadors, The (James),
    9
Ambrose, St., 36
Analects, The (Confucius-
    Pound), 112
Antheil, George, 1
*Antheil and the Treatise on
    Harmony*, 52
Aquinas, St. Thomas, 40, 64
Arnold, Matthew, 12
Articulate Energy (Davie),
    37n, 77n
Atalanta in Calydon (Swin-
    burne), 92
Athenaeum, The, 29

Augustus, 47
"Ayres and Dialogues"
    (Lawes), 52

"Babu English," 25, 54–61
Balzac, Honoré de, 34
Baudelaire, Charles, 73
Beddoes, Thomas Lovell, 7
*Being Geniuses Together
    1920–1930* (McAlmon-
    Boyle), 37n
Bennett, Arnold, 30
Berryman, Jo Brantley, 50n,
    54n
Binyon, Laurence, 105
Bion, 12
"Birks o' Aberfeldy" (Burns),
    92
Blake, William, 7, 8, 22, 23
Blast, xi
Born, Bertrand de, 35
Boyle, Kay, 37n
Bradley, F. H., 41

Brancusi, Constantin, xi, 1
"Briggflatts" (Bunting), 83–84, 85, 93
Browning, Robert, 7, 43, 47–49
Bryan, William Jennings, 112
Buchan, John, 113
Bunting, Basil, 83, 85–88, 93–94
Burns, Robert, 92–93

Caged Panther, The (Meacham), 6n
Camoëns, 12
Campion, Thomas, 61, 86
Camus, Albert, 57
Cantos, The, 2, 14, 18, 49, 62–76, 77–98, 100, 106, 113–14; [1], 92; [20], 72n; [45], 113–14; [47], 79, 92, 94–95; [74], 65, 72–74, 79–80, 81n; [76], 13; [80], 80–81; [81], 81–82, 85–86, 87, 96–98; [85], 81n; [91], 69, 106; [92], 75–76; [95], 76; [110], 82–83; [116], 3–4
"*Cantos, The*" (Davie), 25n
Canzoni, 26, 57n
Carne-Ross, D. S., 17n, 45n
"Castle Boterel" (Hardy), 46
Cathay, 36, 37
Catherine the Great, 111
Catullus, 25–26, 35, 37–38, 44
"Catullus: XXXI" (Hardy), 26n
Celebration of Charis: in Ten Lyric Pieces, A (Jonson), 78
Chace, William, 118
Charles Olson (ed. Corrigan), 22n

Chaucer, Geoffrey, 23, 24, 60, 86, 96–98
"Chercheuses de Poux, Les" (Rimbaud), 39
Chesterton, G.K., 71
Chinese Poetry in English Verse (Giles), 36n
"Chinese Written Character as a Medium for Poetry, The" (Fenollosa), 77n
Chopin, Frédéric, 91
Ciung Iung, L'Asse Che Non Vacilla (Confucius-Pound), 81n
Cobban, A., 112n
Cocteau, Jean, xi, 1
Coleridge, Samuel T., 14
Collected Poems of Thomas Hardy, The, 26n
Collignon, Raymonde, 50–51, 85
Confucius, 2, 42, 81n, 110, 112
Confucius to Cummings (ed. Pound-Spann), 45n, 46n, 93
Connolly, Thomas E., 52
Conquest, Robert, 57
"Conversation between Ezra Pound and Allen Ginsberg, A" (Reck), 4n
Cookson, William, 7n, 113n
Cooper, James Fenimore, 7
Corbière, Tristan, 38, 39
Corrigan, Matthew, 22n
Corrigan, Robert A., 17n, 37n
Cory, Daniel, 3n
Cournos, John, 37n
Crabbe, George, 8, 35, 39
Crick, F. H. C., 67
Crowning Privilege, The (Graves), 57n
Curie, Marie, 66n

Daniel, Arnaud, 13, 104

Dante, 12, 35, 49, 73, 81*n*, 92, 103–106

Davie, Donald, 25*n*, 37*n*, 50*n*, 56*n*, 58*n*, 77*n*

Debussy, Claude, 46

Dickens, Charles, 34

Dickinson, Emily, 7

Diderot, Denis, 111

Discretions (Rachewiltz), 81*n*, 119

Discussions of Poetry (ed. Murphy), 38*n*

Divine Comedy, The (Dante), 64, 103–106

Dolmetsch, Arnold, 52, 82, 85, 96

Donne, John, 86, 102

Doolittle, Hilda ("H. D."), 27, 32

Doria, Charles, 21–22

Dostoevski, Feodor, 13

Dowland, John, 82, 85, 86, 98

Dryden, John, 102, 119, 120

Dudek, Louis, 3, 4

Duhamel, Georges, 45

Dürer, Albrecht, 24

"Elegy" (Gray), 54

Eliot, T. S., xi, xii, 1, 2, 5, 27–30, 32, 38, 40, 41, 53, 88–89, 91, 104, 111, 116

Encyclopédie de la musique et Dictionnaire du Conservatoire (Laurencie-Lavignac), 90

Endymion (Keats), 61

English Review, 17*n*, 46

"Envoi," 50–52

Epipsychidion (Shelley), 15

Epoca, 2, 4

Epstein, Sir Jacob, 1

Espey, J. J., 54*n*, 58*n*

Euripides, 90

Europe and the French Revolution (Sorel), 112*n*

"Experimental School in American Poetry, The" (Winters), 38*n*

Exultations, 11, 17

"Ezra Pound" (Cory), 3*n*

Ezra Pound (Norman), 6*n*

Ezra Pound (ed. Sullivan), 17*n*

"Ezra Pound and the Ostriches" (Homberger), 7*n*

"Ezra Pound and Thomas Hardy" (Hutchins), 43*n*

Ezra Pound and Sextus Propertius (Sullivan), 57*n*, 58*n*

Ezra Pound: His Metric and Poetry (Eliot), 40

Ezra Pound: Poet as Sculptor (Davie), 50*n*, 56*n*, 58*n*

Ezra Pound: Poetics for an Electric Age (Nänny), 5*n*

Ezra Pound: Selected Prose 1909–1965 (ed. Cookson), 7*n*, 113*n*

"Ezra Pound's 'Hugh Selwyn Mauberley'" (Davie), 50*n*

Ezra Pound's Kensington (Hutchins), 6*n*

Ezra Pound's Mauberley (Espey), 54*n*

Fabre, Jean Henri, 66*n*

Fanon, Frantz, 13, 57

Fenollosa, Ernest F., 36, 77*n*

"Few Don'ts for an Imagist, A," 32–33

Fielding, Henry, 8

"Figlia Che Piange, La" (Eliot), 27

"Flame, The," 26

Flaubert, Gustave, 7, 24, 34–35

Flint, F. S., 33*n*

Fontenelle, Bernard de, 8

Ford, Ford Madox, xi, 9, 31, 34–35, 46, 48

Four Quartets (Eliot), 89

Frederick the Great, 111

Freud, Sigmund, 13

Frobenius, Leo, 66*n*, 108

Frost, Robert, 32

Fuller, Buckminster, 68

Function of Criticism, The (Winters), 75*n*

"Further Notes on Mauberley" (Connolly), 52*n*

Fussell, Edwin, 23*n*, 24

Gaudier-Brzeska, Henri, 1, 37, 40

Gaudier-Brzeska: A Memoir, 40–41

Gautier, Théophile, 7, 39, 41, 54

Georgian Poetry (ed. Marsh), 31

Gifford, William, 61

Giles, Herbert Allen, 36

Gissing, George, 30

"Going, The" (Hardy), 46

Goldsmith, Oliver, 108

Gosse, Sir Edmund, 9, 30

Gourmont, Remy de, 7, 66*n*

Graves, Robert, 57

Gray, Thomas, 54

Green Helmet, The (Yeats), 40

Guide to Kulchur, 44, 48, 65, 109

"Gypsy, The," 37–38

Hale, William Gardner, 56*n*

Hardy, Thomas, 7, 9*n*, 24, 43–49, 50, 53, 90–91, 94, 118

Hawthorne, Nathaniel, 7, 24

Heine, Heinrich, 7

Hemingway, Ernest, xi, 1, 13

"Her Triumph" (Jonson), 78, 84–85, 87

Herbert, George, 86

Hesternae Rosae (Rummel), 51*n*

Hewlett, Maurice, 15, 99

History of Chinese Literature (Giles), 36*n*

Hitler, Adolf, 110

Hokusai, Katsushika, 24

"Homage à Rameau" (Debussy), 46

Homage to Sextus Propertius, 44, 46–48, 54–61, 91

Homberger, Eric, 7

Homer, 104

Horace, 35

Hugh Selwyn Mauberley, 9, 37, 44, 49–54, 86, 88–89

Hughes, Glenn, 32*n*

Hulme, T. E., 1, 9, 32, 34

Humboldt, Baron Alexander von, 66*n*

Hunt, J. W., 112*n*

Hutchins, Patricia, 6*n*, 44*n*

Ibsen, Henrik, 13

Imaginary Letters, 53

Imagism, 31–41

Imagism and the Imagists (Hughes), 32*n*

"Imagisme" (Pound-Flint), 33*n*

In Defense of Reason (Winters), 38*n*

"In Durance," 14–16, 18

"In Tenebris III" (Hardy), 90

Instigations, 77n, 88n
Irving, Washington, 24

James, Henry, 9n, 23, 24,
  49, 111, 116
Jefferson, Thomas, 8, 25, 111
Jefferson and/or Mussolini,
  111
Jenkyns, John, 82, 85, 96
"Jewel Stairs' Grievance,
  The," 37
Johnson, Samuel, 48, 64
Jonson, Ben, 38, 60, 78, 84–
  88, 95–97, 119
Joyce, James, xi, 1, 25, 32
Jude the Obscure (Hardy),
  44

Keats, John, 61, 119, 120
Kenner, Hugh, 68, 81n, 108
Kipling, Rudyard, 55
Knox, Bryant, 42n
Kora in Hell (Williams), 27
Korg, Jacob, 49n

Laforgue, Jules, 38
Landor, Walter Savage, 7,
  49, 60
Lattimore, Richard, 57n
Laurencie, Lionel de la, 90
Lavignac, Albert, 90
Lawes, Henry, 51, 52–53, 85,
  96
Leopardi, Giacomo, 7
Leopold (of Tuscany), 111
*Letters of Ezra Pound, 1907–
  1941, The* (ed. Paige), 72n
*Letters of Wyndham Lewis,
  The* (ed. Rose), 119n
Levi, Grazia, 2–3
Lewis, Percy Wyndham, xi,
  1, 28, 29, 31, 32, 42, 43,
  46, 60, 68, 118–19

Life of Ezra Pound, The
  (Stock), 6n, 118
*Literary Essays of Ezra
  Pound, The* (ed. Eliot),
  33n
Little Review, The, 77n
Longinus, 65
Lope de Vega, xi, 12
"Love Song of J. Alfred
  Prufrock, The" (Eliot), 41
Lovelace, Richard, 85, 86
Lowell, Amy, 32
Lucifer in Harness (Fussell),
  23n
Lustra, 2, 36n, 37, 49, 58n

McAlmon, Robert, 36n–37n
McLuhan, Marshall, 5
Mallarmé, Stéphane, 31, 40
Manning, Frederic, 9
Marsh, Sir Edward, 31
Martial, 35, 37, 38
Marvell, Andrew, 86
Masefield, John, 99, 100
Maximus Poems (Olson), 85
Meacham, Harry M., 6n
Mead, G. R. S., 9, 68
"Medallion," 50, 54n
Melville, Herman, 7, 34
Mencius, 42
Metastasio, 8
Milton, John, 23, 24, 102,
  119
Modern Age, The (ed. Ford),
  50n
Monroe, Harriet, 56n
Moore, Marianne, 32
Moschus, 12
Murger, Henri, 28
Murphy, F. E. X., 38n
"Music of Lost Dynasties,
  The" (Korg), 49n
Mussolini, Benito, 62, 64,
  110–111

Nänny, Max, 5

Natural Philosophy of Love, The (Gourmont-Pound), 66*n*

"Near Perigord," 49

New Age, The, 18, 50, 57*n*, 72*n*, 94

"New Metres for Old" (Carne-Ross), 45*n*

New Word, The (Upward), 42, 54, 64*n*, 66, 71, 111*n*

Nichols, Robert, 57, 60–61

Nietzsche, Friedrich, 13

Nobel, Alfred, 54, 56, 66

Norman, Charles, 6*n*

Notes sur la technique poétique (Duhamel-Vildrac), 45

Notes Toward the Definition of Culture (Eliot), 116

Observer, The, 60

"Ode to Augustus" (Pope), 48

Oliver Cromwell (Buchan), 113

Olson, Charles, 85, 92, 94

"On the Principles of Genial Criticism" (Coleridge), 14

Open Poetry (Quasha), 7*n*

Orage, A. R., 18

Paideuma, 6*n*, 17*n*, 25*n*, 37*n*, 42*n*, 50*n*, 58*n*, 81*n*

Paige, D. D., 72*n*

Paradis Artificiels, Les (Baudelaire), 73

Paradiso (Dante), 105

Patria Mia, 18–19, 23–24, 28, 94

Peachy, Frederic, 57*n*

Peck, John, 116*n*

Penguin Book of Modern Translated Verse (ed. Steiner), 59*n*

Periods of European Literature (Saintsbury), 12

Personae, 11, 14, 16, 17

Physique de L'amour (Gourmont), 66*n*

Picabia, Francis, 1

Pisan Cantos, The, xii, 13, 48, 65, 72 74, 79 82, 85 86, 87, 96 98

Plato, 64

Poema del Cid, 12

Poems of 1912 13 Satires of Circumstance (Hardy), 46

Poetry, 33*n*, 56*n*, 88*n*

"Poetry and Mr. Pound" (Nichols), 57*n*

Polite Essays, 92

Pope, Alexander, 48, 102

Pound, Dorothy, xi, xii

Pound, Ezra, *passim*; anti-Semitism of, 4, 19, 23, 94, 101, 112; biographical chronology of, xi–xii; bohemianism of, 28–29, 31; Browning influence on, 47–49; and Chinese culture, 13, 36, 41–42, 108–10; and classicism, 21–22, 25, 35, 37–38, 39, 44–45, 55–61, 71, 90, 107–108; and Eliot, 28–30, 32, 40, 53, 89; Europeanism of, 17–22; and fascism, 13, 23, 81*n*, 110–13; language of, 11–18, 25–26, 32 41, 51–61, 69–70, 103–104, 119 20; letters to Hardy, 43–49, 53, 118; and "literary civilization," 100 110, 113–17; and literary movements, 30–42; and mask or persona, 53–54, 119; Mediterranean cul-

ture of, 11–14, 35, 55–56, 101, 108–10; and modernism, 5, 7–9, 24, 52; and music, 36, 39–40, 50–53, 85, 92–93, 98, 101–102; and nature of "idea" in *Cantos*, 63–76; prosody of, 45, 84–98, 101–102; relation to America, 18–25, 52, 111–12; and scholarships, 5–6, 106–108; self-accusations of, 2–5
"Pound and Lewis" (Rose), 28n, 94n
Pound Era, The (Kenner), 68n
Pound Newsletter, The, 56n, 57n
"Pound, Olson, and the Classical Tradition" (Doria), 22n
"Prayer for His Lady's Life," 57n
Projective Verse (Olson), 92
Propertius, Sextus, 47, 58n, 60, 61
Prufrock and Other Observations (Eliot), 88

Quarterly Review, 61
Quasha, George, 7n, 8n
Querschnitt, Der, 116n
Quinzaine for this Yule, A, 17

Rachewiltz, Boris de, 108
Rachewiltz, Mary de, 80n–81n, 119
Rameau, Jean Philippe, 46
Read, Sir Herbert, 28n
Reading the Cantos (Stock), 36n
Reck, Michael, 4n
"Remy de Gourmont," 7n

Rennert, Hugo, xi
"Retrospect, A," 33n
Rimbaud, Arthur, 39
Ring and the Book, The (Browning), 49
Rock-Drill, 69, 75–76
Roosevelt, F. D., 62, 64
Rose, W. K., 28n, 36n, 42n, 94n, 119n
Rossetti, Dante Gabriel, 7, 15
Rowlandson, Thomas, 60
Rummel, Walter Morse, 51

Saintsbury, George, 9, 12, 13, 17, 108
Sassoon, Siegfried, 29
Scènes de la Vie de Bohème (Murger), 28
"Scholars, The" (Yeats), 107
Shakespear, Dorothy: *see* Pound, Dorothy
Shakespeare, William, 104, 119, 120
Shaw, George Bernard, 71
Shelley, Percy Bysshe, 15
Shepherd, William Pierce, xi
So Long to Learn (Masefield), 99
Social Credit: An Impact, xii
Song of Roland, The, 12
"Song of the Bowmen of Shu," 37
Sophocles, 56
Sordello, 49
Sordello (Browning), 49
Sorel, Albert, 112n
Spann, Marcella, 45n
Spenser, Edmund, 23, 24
Spirit of Romance, The, 11–12, 18, 53, 92, 105
Stalin, Joseph, 110
Steiner, George, 59n

Stendhal, 7, 34
"Stepping Westwards"
    (Wordsworth), 37*n*
Stevens, Wallace, 18
Stevenson, R. L., 99
Stock, Noel, 6*n*, 36*n*, 118
Sullivan, J. P., 17*n*, 33*n*,
    45*n*, 57*n*, 58*n*
Swinburne, A. C., 7, 92
Symbolism, 30–31, 38–41
*Symbolist Movement in
    Literature, The*
    (Symons), 30, 38
Symons, Arthur, 30, 31, 38

*Testament of François
    Villon, The*, xii
"These Be Your Gods"
    (Graves), 57*n*
Thomas, Edward, 16–17
Thoreau, Henry David, 7
Thucydides, 21
Times Literary Supplement,
    29
Trachiniae (Sophocles),
    56*n*
"Treatise on Metre," 88, 89–
    90
Turgenev, Ivan, 24, 34
"Two Poets" (Thomas), 17*n*

Under the Greenwood Tree
    (Hardy), 9, 119
Unwobbling Pivot, The
    (Confucius-Pound), 81*n*,
    110
Upward, Allen, 9, 25, 41–42,
    54–56, 58, 63–72, 74–75,
    111*n*

Valéry, Paul, 40
Van Dyke, Henry, 23
"Vanity of Human Wishes,
    The" (Johnson), 48, 64

Velazquez, Diego de Silva y,
    24
Verlaine, Paul, 30, 99
Vildrac, Charles, 45
Villon, François, 12, 13, 14,
    35, 53
Vision, A (Yeats), 68
"Voice, The" (Hardy), 46
Voltaire, 8, 108, 111
Vorticism, 31–32, 36, 40,
    41–42, 66–67

Waller, Edmund, 52–53, 82,
    85, 86, 98, 102
Wanderings of Oisin, The
    (Yeats), 30–31
Watson, James D., 67
Wells, H. G., 30
"What I feel about Walt
    Whitman," 23*n*
Whigham, Peter, 37, 38
Whistler, James McNeill, 7
    8, 24, 27–28, 30
Whitman, Walt, 18, 23, 24
Wilamowitz-Moellendorff,
    Ulrich, 21
Williams, William Carlos, 1,
    27, 94
Winckelmann, J. J., 21
Wind among the Reeds, The
    (Yeats), 9, 30, 35
Winters, Yvor, 38*n*, 75
Women of Trachis
    (Sophocles-Pound), 56
Wordsworth, William, 37*n*,
    60

Yeats, William Butler, xi,
    xii, 1, 9*n*, 30, 34–35, 38,
    40, 53, 60, 65, 68, 104,
    107, 109

Zola, Emile, 30